Quitting Cold Stone
(And Other Struggles)

Sam Neumann

Copyright © 2013 Top Drawer Publishing

All rights reserved.

ALSO BY SAM NEUMANN

*Memoirs of a Gas Station:
A Delightfully Awkward Journey Across
the Alaskan Tundra*

CONTENTS

Acknowledgments	i
Three Days in September	1
The Quitter	8
Why I Am Condescending to the Automated Call System Lady	14
"Happy Birthday. Have a Great One!"	21
The Road to Branson	25
Dear Parking Services	35
Defending Nickelback	39
Mother Nature is a Tramp	45
To the Guy Who Leaves His Grocery Cart in the Middle of the Parking Lot	51
All Overrated List, Part 1	55
All Underrated List, Part 1	61
A Man Named Plaxico	65
The First Day of School	70
The Wonders of Bob Ross	75
The Tipping Point	80

I'm Feeling Skinny, Tony	83
Status Abuse	87
Your Sport Preference Offends Me	92
Confessions of a Wi-Fi Thief	97
Foie Gras Reduction	105
Five Thoughts on John Mayer	109
Ode to Audi	120
Wasting Your Vote	125
The Stages of the Dog	132
The Best Defense Against Assholes	137
All Overrated List, Part 2	141
All Underrated List, Part 2	147
Customer Service By Comcast	152
Some Thoughts on the Election	161
What is the Deal With Airline Travel?	164

Acknowledgments

Thanks to Kristen, Josi, Jo, and Donna for their invaluable input on various stages of this book. And thanks to Jim for all his design advice and for, even after all the incendiary things I wrote about him in my previous book, somehow resisting the urge to strangle me to death.

THREE DAYS IN SEPTEMBER

It was autumn of 2006, the year of our Lord. I was a sophomore in college, desperately trying to gain weight and make sense of the town of Ames, Iowa. Neither came easily. With year two came large scale changes; gone were the dorms, the never-ending food supply at the campus feeding trough (sometimes referred to as the "dining hall"), and the one-year grace period of not really having to work because I was, you know, getting acclimated. I resided in a house off campus and commuted to class via a purple moped I'd bought second hand. The meal-plan was a thing of the past, the money had dried up, and I needed a job.

Now technically, I had a job. I was a reporter for the Iowa State Daily, brazenly following my lifelong dream of becoming a sportswriter. It was going average at best, mostly because I was beginning to discover I didn't really like it, and I wasn't very good at it either. Put those two things together, and I started to question the inevitable success I'd been expecting up to that point. How bad was I? In my two years of covering the women's golf team (yet another indicator I wasn't quite punching my ticket to the big time), I never once met the head coach in person. Or any of the players, for that matter. Somehow I still managed to turn out stories at a reasonable clip and avoid getting fired.

The problem with this job wasn't my general incompetence or absence of drive; it was the pay, or lack thereof. I was getting compensated per story, but the amount was so nominal it barely covered my Friday night post-drinking Burger King intake. For this reason, I needed a real job. *Who knows,* I thought, *maybe I'll even find something I don't hate.*

I began looking through Iowa State's online job database, and soon found a description that matched my core values:

Looking for a self-starter. Ideal candidate is a quick learner and enjoys working in a fast-paced environment. Must be enthusiastic and energetic. Needs to be available weekends.

Well sure, that sounded like me! I was born to work in a fast-paced environment, and all that other shit could surely be learned. The job was for a Cold Stone Creamery that had recently opened. I'd never been to one, but had heard they had good ice cream. Good enough for me. I applied for the opening among dozens of others – the clichéd throwing a bunch of stuff against the wall and hoping something sticks. Well, exactly one thing stuck, and wouldn't you know it, it was the Cold Stone gig. I went in for the interview, killed it (i.e. had a pulse and working appendages), and soon I was a proud member of the team.

A few days before my debut, I got an email from Steve, the manager, politely directing me to the company website to watch some tutorials and learn about the company's history before my first day. I grinned at the thought. Homework? He actually expected me to do homework for a stopgap minimum-wage job? How adorable. I wrote it off as a formality that nobody actually completed, and never thought about it again.

Day One came, and I learned I was mistaken about the

formality part. Before anything else, Steve took me aside and drilled me on everything I was supposed to have learned. Occasionally I got a word out in response, but for the most part my mouth just hung open and made confused creaking noises. I hadn't expected this. Irritated with me already, Steve commanded me to go home and study harder. "Also," he said in closing, "learn the first seven songs."

Songs? Ah yes, I'd heard of this. Cold Stone employees were required to sing some sort of bastardized ice cream version of a nursery rhyme every time they were tipped. According to lore, the tipping didn't happen often, and thus the songs were few and far between. Still, it seemed a little demeaning. I guess I understood this going into it, but it hadn't been quite so real until I got there. I was beginning to wonder about this job.

Two days passed and I was in a bad place. Ames was deserted – the student body had migrated to Iowa City that weekend for the annual Iowa/Iowa State football game, as was customary every other year when the game was played on The University of Iowa's campus. I, of course, had to work at my new job over the weekend and was stuck in Ames by myself. How shitty. And even shittier, I was finding out, was the job itself.

My first two days had not gone well. After my failed interrogation, I learned how to wash dishes and clean the infamous "cold stone" on which the ice cream treats were made. I did get a free treat after each shift, but that was the only redeeming factor. The pace was frantic, the management overbearing, and the hours were long – each night we didn't leave until after midnight. The uniforms were embarrassing and the songs were plentiful – much more prevalent than I'd expected, yet somehow the nightly tip total to be divided among the crew made my per-article rate at the Daily look like a fortune. I was generally allowed to abstain from singing, for I was still learning the songs, but it was made clear the grace period wouldn't last much longer. Soon I'd have to sing.

Around noon on Saturday – a full eight hours before my shift started – I got a phone call from a man named Solberg. A good friend from high school who resided in Minneapolis, I hadn't expected to hear from him on that particular day.

"Neumann," came his voice through the phone, "where do you live?"

"Um," I said confused, for he already knew the answer, "Ames, Iowa."

"No, like specifically where do you live? What's your address? We're in Ames right now. We came to visit you."

That sly son of a bitch. He and two other high school friends had driven the four hours without telling me. A classic surprise, for which I was grateful, but also slightly apprehensive; I did, after all, have to work that evening, and I didn't want to spoil any impromptu parties.

I explained this to the three of them when they arrived at my door. I also explained the weekend vibe might not be super awesome, because of the mass student exodus that had taken place – you could almost hear the crickets during daytime hours. They didn't seem overly concerned about either of these things, and promptly found their way to the fridge to crack a few Natural Lights. We drank and played yard games for the next five hours. Over the course of the afternoon, the details of the job came out.

"So," Preston (Friend #2) said with a skeptical look, "Cold Stone, huh?"

"Yeah, I mean, I needed a job," I told him. "It's money." I looked at the ground.

"Do you like it?"

I paused for a second and fought an internal battle; do I try to justify it to them – and myself – or do I tell the truth? I chose the truth.

"No, it actually kind of sucks."

QUITTING COLD STONE (AND OTHER STRUGGLES)

By the time evening came, it had all come out: I hated the job and didn't want to work there anymore. But I needed money, so that was my driving factor. After I told them this, the boys (and girl) spent the next few hours gradually trying to convince me to quit.

"Neumann," they'd say, "I mean, we drove down here. You're not actually going in tonight are you?"

"I have to. I can't miss a shift this early on."

"Why the hell not? You don't even want to work there."

"Yeah but I can't get fired. That looks bad on a resume."

"Well, just quit then."

And there was the rub. No matter what argument I gave, it always ended with that response: just quit then. And I must admit they made a compelling point. Why would I ruin a perfectly good Saturday with the gang from high school for some shit job I didn't even like? I mentioned something about two weeks' notice at one point, which they quickly dismissed with a scoff. "Nobody actually does that. That's more of a suggestion."

Still not convinced I'd actually go through with it – I was quite the straight-laced lad, if you can tell – we entertained countless scenarios of how I'd actually do the quitting. Probably the most convoluted was the plan that had Preston impersonating me; he would dress up in my uniform and tell the boss that he (I) was quitting. He would have a hat on and we had similar body types, and after only two days, my coworkers weren't that familiar with my looks, so it seemed like it could've been borderline passable and not completely crazy. But in the end, we went with a more conventional approach: I would confront Steve, blabber something about how I just had so much on my plate, was overwhelmed with school, and it just wasn't possible for me to work weekends. All total lies, but it sounded good. Since the ability to work weekends was a term of my initial employment, Steve would insist that was what they needed me to do, we would come to a stalemate, and the only option would be for me to end my professional relationship with Cold Stone Creamery. The split would be amicable and mutual. I wouldn't feel that bad.

The time came and I strapped on my hat and apron and went in. I was nervous, for I'd never done this before. For the first 15 minutes of my shift, I washed dishes in the back while I tried to work up the courage. Steve eventually came back to check on me.

"Everything going alright?" He could sense my unrest. I turned around halfway and gave him the spiel without once looking up from the sink. I made sure to stress at the end how much I just couldn't do weekends with my busy schedule, and waited for his counter.

"No problem," he said pleasantly. "We'll just have you do weekdays."

Well shit. There went my out. I froze, not knowing what to do next. The entire plan was contingent upon him disagreeing with me about the weekend thing. How would I ever get out now? I would have to retire at Cold Stone.

"That being said," Steve continued, "have you seen enough that...maybe you don't want to work here anymore?"

It was a lifeline; a clear path to freedom served on a platter for me. I couldn't believe it. Still, it took me at least ten seconds to respond. I was very, very bad at this.

"You know," I said through a clenched jaw, "I think so."

And it was done. I turned in my hat and apron – Cold Stone equivalent of gun and badge – and exited the premises not 30 minutes after I'd entered. A wave of total freedom washed over me and I congratulated myself on doing something that wasn't actually that hard, but for a clean-cut, easily guilted American boy like myself, seemed nearly impossible. I met the gang back at the house, where they greeted me with shots of booze, frozen pizza, and big smiles. It was over. I was free. I had done something not completely upstanding. And it felt awesome.

THE QUITTER

The Cold Stone debacle is, I suppose, a suitable introduction to who I am. In the previous passage I wrote of the uncomfortable shame I felt for bailing on the job in the fashion I did, because I was an alleged "good kid." This is true – I did feel those things, and I was for the most part "good" – but I was only troubled by the specifics of the situation; peer pressure, on-the-spot confrontation, and the unknown that lied ahead. The quitting itself was not really an issue – subconsciously I was probably planning to quit, because quitting is kind of what I do. I quit stuff all the time.

Whatever it says about me as a person, I've become very comfortable with bailing on stuff right smack in the middle of whatever it is I'm supposed to be doing. It's probably because it happened so frequently in my formative years; I made quitting activities a habit growing up and had no real remorse about it. In the beginning, sure, I felt a little dumb, but the more times I cut and ran, the more normal it became.

It started with the nature class. I couldn't have been older than seven, and I was signed up for a summer community education course that explored the wonders of the natural world, with a specific focus on insects. It was part of a summer program for kids and teens in the Chisago Lakes, Minn., area, probably to take them off their tired parents' hands for a few days. Being a young boy, I was obviously fascinated by bugs, so it seemed like a perfect fit.

Except for the fact that I actually had to go. You see, at this age I had developed quite the system in the summertime, one so fine I struggle to understand why it was ever replaced. Being the fact that school was out of session, the framework of my daily life was remarkably open-ended – I had literally zero commitments. So the system, of course, was doing whatever the hell I wanted. When a variable was introduced – even one that was agreeable on the surface, like an awesome bug seminar – it threw the entire sequence out of whack. I liked to decide what I would do and when I would do it. If I was being required to be somewhere, then I lost control of that. Someone else was calling the shots, and that did not fit in to my scheme.

So I went to the nature class for a day or two and naturally hated it. The content was actually pretty boss – basically walking in the woods looking for insects – but that didn't matter. It was required, there were assignments (probably no more than bringing in a used milk carton for a moss trap or something, but still assignments), and I was uncomfortable, dammit. These were strange people in a strange place. The age range of the kids involved was varied, so that meant there were some older boys, who were loud, boisterous, and probably intimidating on these nature walks. What the hell was this about? Why should I have to hang out with these assholes?

I returned to my mother's minivan after the second day and informed her I wouldn't be attending anymore. She asked why, and while there was surely a conversation, it boiled down to one simple explanation: I didn't wanna.

From then on, I enjoyed making my own schedule, and was again within my comfort zone. Outside the obvious commitment of school, which was kind of hard to avoid, I kept my engagements to a minimum and was extremely content. Why give up the freedom of youth?

This system worked until I reached the age where kids are sort of expected to start actually doing stuff. Around junior high, I suppose, I was expected to begin playing sports or joining the marching band or glee club. This didn't seem daunting to me, probably because I had avoided actual commitment for so long I forgot what it felt like. So when seventh grade rolled around, I joined the football team along with most other boys in my class. It was the first year kids were allowed to play real, tackle football, and it was just kind of assumed every adolescent would do it. We practiced or played games every day after school, and I despised it. People kept referencing "having fun" in regard to the sport, but I had no idea what the hell they were talking about. It wasn't that I minded the sport itself – I rather liked football – but being required to give up my free time to put on a helmet and pads and run into other youngsters every afternoon? It didn't seem like the best use of my life.

This, however, is what I was required to do, so I struggled through one season of seventh-grade football, often plotting how I'd bail but never pulling the trigger. Perhaps I needed an intervention from Solberg and Preston. I played tight end and mostly blocked; the team threw two passes to the tight end all year, and both went to the other guy who played the position. Both were also intercepted. On defense I played defensive back and tallied one tackle.

After this triumphant year, I halfheartedly signed on for the next season of pigskin. Knowing what I was up against, I had no real desire to be on the team, but again it was just kind of expected. Plus, it was that or get a job.

A week or so into fall practice it all fell apart. I begrudgingly entered the locker room one day after school to suit up for another afternoon of organized team activities, only to find that all of my equipment had been mixed up with someone else's and was now unaccounted for. While this may seem like a minor setback, it was just the discouragement I needed to go ahead and call it a career; in my mind, the equipment thing was such a debacle that it would be easier to quit than to find new gear. I also remember having serious trouble finding rides home after practice, but the details of this are hazy. Regardless, these two factors pushed me to tender my resignation letter to my teacher and coach, Mr. Chrun. He was remarkably unbothered by my departure, but then again 'ol Chrun didn't get worked up about much of anything.

Freshman year of high school arrived and I was, like a moron, considering joining the football team again. I figured I'd matured in the past year and with a newborn commitment to the sport I could really make this work. I was of course wrong. The plan was actually ill-fated from the start, as I entered fall camp with a load of torn cartilage in my right ankle (the result of an unrelated rock-jumping accident). It was undiagnosed at the time; the doctors had just told me I had a sprain. But it lingered much longer than a sprain would, and all I knew was my ankle hurt and I couldn't really run well.

I simply assumed the ankle would improve with time and decided to suit up anyway. Idiot. The first two weeks were a living hell – two-a-day practices in 90-degree heat and humidity can be a struggle for even the fittest youth, and a borderline nightmare for a lanky undersized freshman with a limp. I plodded through the drills and meetings until my coach pulled me aside during a morning practice.

"Neumann," he said. "It's killing me to watch you run."

"Well, coach, I have a..."

"I know. It's absolutely killing me. I think what we should do is have you sit out the rest of this morning, then take the afternoon practice off. Then we'll see how you feel, and figure out where to go from there."

"Where we went from there" was once again off the

QUITTING COLD STONE (AND OTHER STRUGGLES)

football team. The ankle did not get any better, and I realized that my football playing potential was quite limited, even when healthy. When I was broken, it made no sense to continue. I quit. And for once, I never returned.

The football team and bug class are just a few examples; there have been far too many other desertions to list. Summer jobs? Quit. Church groups? Stop showing up. After-school activities? Cut and run. College clubs? Fucking bailed.

Why? Why did I so often start things and fail to follow through? I'm not sure; my father did his best to instill a solid work ethic in me, and for the most part I've been able to stick with the things that actually matter – high school, college, and real (paying) jobs. But aside from that, I could justify removing myself from something if the tangible gain wasn't apparent. If I wasn't enjoying it (which I almost universally wasn't), and if it wasn't paying obvious dividends (and didn't have the potential to do so in the foreseeable future), I didn't see the point in wasting my time. I had other stuff to do, like build tree forts and make rafts out of cardboard and duct tape. I certainly had something against commitment, but I didn't withdraw myself from activity completely – I still *did* things, but just things on my time, rather than when someone else was telling me to do them. Being forced to do something always took the fun out of it for me.

So I used the time I would've been sweating it out on the football practice field to construct a four-level mansion in the woods, or conduct a thorough investigation – complete with a case file and evidence bags – of the curious cigarette butts that were found on the porch that belonged to my non-smoking family. I also played video games, but a man needs some leisure from time to time, right? Right?

The point is this: organized activities aren't for everyone. Some of us need to do things in our own way, on our own time, and as long as we're still *doing* something, that's okay. I'm obviously one of these people, and that's why I write, and why I'm writing this book. Writing is on my time, just as reading is on your time, and neither of them involve tackling dummies. Antisocial? Maybe. But writing is where I ended up when I stopped doing what I was supposed to do and started doing what I wanted to do, and so far it's gone alright. Given my history, I guess there's a chance I'll bail on this book before it's finished, but I think the fact that I'm still here bodes well. The seeds of a flake-out are usually planted early.

I can tell you I definitely probably won't bail on this book, and I hope you won't either. I promise I won't make you show up to any insect classes.

WHY I AM CONDESCENDING TO THE AUTOMATED CALL SYSTEM LADY

"Press 1 for English," she used to say. This part never bothered me – it's just pressing a number, which isn't difficult or even inconvenient. These days, however, it's getting awfully dicey.

Ever since the automated voice menu ladies of the world banded together and decided they'd like to have conversations with us, things have gotten steadily worse. For awhile they were content with just guiding us through a series of prompts that required the caller to press buttons, which would inevitably lead to one of the following:

a) We eventually got the answer we desired.

b) We were allowed to speak with a real human (the proverbial light at the end of the tunnel).

c) We got frustrated enough to throw the phone across the room.

I suspect number three happened most often, but regardless, I was down with this method. Nobody likes these automated menus, which as a rule require at least 10 minutes of hold time somewhere along the line, but at times they are a necessary evil. And punching buttons just seems like the best way to go about it – it reiterates the fact that you are indeed dealing with a machine and nothing more. It's not trying to be anything it's not. Button punching keeps it real.

But no. That wasn't enough. While some calling systems have retained their button punching ways (and God bless them for it), the majority have decided we'd rather talk than press 1. Now, for English, we say "English." Somehow this is supposed to make us happier. You can almost hear the execs that came up with this scheme in the background – "See! They said 'English' and the machine understood it! It's amazing. It's like they're having a conversation with a real person! The 21st century has arrived! We are titans of industry!!!" While they're clearly elated with this innovation, I do not share the enthusiasm.

It starts out cool. "Oh, look at that, I said the word and the machine understood it. Not bad. That was way easier than pressing a button. Wait, was it?" But before I can make a decision on the matter, we are on to the next topic, which sometimes requires multiple words or even full sentences. The machine woman starts to struggle, even when I'm enunciating to the best of my abilities, and she often simply responds with an "I'm sorry, I didn't understand. Can you repeat that?" Her voice is calm and friendly, but I don't care. I'm pissed at this point – the bitch isn't hearing me, and I shouldn't have to repeat what I just said in a perfectly clear manner. This is when I get attitude with her.

The key here – the key in any automated voice menu situation – is resisting that urge to send the phone sailing through the window and into the front yard. And the way I do this is by getting condescending. If I'm an asshole to this woman, it somehow makes me feel better and grants me the strength to continue the conversation. It sometimes even helps with her comprehension. I know she can't understand my inflection, and thus is un-phased by

QUITTING COLD STONE (AND OTHER STRUGGLES)

my scathing tone, but I'd like to believe that I'm hurting her feelings just a little, machine or not. An example of one of these conversations is as follows:

Automated Voice Lady: For English, please say "English."

Me: Only because you said please. English.

AVL: I'm sorry, I didn't understand. Can you repeat that?

Me: English.

AVL: Okay, your call will continue in English. Now, what can I help you with? Please say the reason for your call. For example, you can say "account information" or "order checks."

Me: I want to open a savings account.

AVL: Okay, I can help you order checks. First, say the number of boxes of checks you would like. For example, you can say "five" or "ten."

Me: Zero.

AVL: I'm sorry, I didn't understand. Please say the number of boxes of checks you would like. For example, you can say "five" or "ten."

Me: I don't want any checks you dumb cow. I said savings account. SAVINGS ACCOUNT.

AVL: I'm sorry, I didn't understand. Do you want to order checks? If so, say "yes." If not, say "something else."

Me: (scoff) Something ELSE.

AVL: Okay, something else. Please say what I can help you with. For example, you can say "account information" or "order checks."

Me: Fucking savings account. Same thing I said before.

AVL: I heard "check balance on account." Is this correct? Please say "yes" or "no."

Me: Um, *no*.

AVL: Okay, something else. Please say what I can help you with. For example...

Me: Can I just talk to a damn person? One without wax

in her ears?

AVL: I heard "balance transfer." Is this correct? Please say "yes" or "no."

Me: You tell me.

AVL: I'm sorry, I didn't understand. If you would like to talk to a customer service specialist, please press zero.

Me: Yes! A button! (punches zero)

And really, that's all I wanted the whole time – to speak to a real person and/or press a button. Of course, there was the mandatory 10-minute hold period, but compared to dealing with Helen Keller over there, that part was a breeze. Sometimes you have to play the game.

GOOD FAT/BAD FAT

We are a world of good and bad. Black and white. Democrat and Republican. Our team and their team. There's really no way around it; we deal in absolutes. While this is generally wrong and an unrefined way of thinking, it's what we do. Indeed, *the answer lies somewhere in between* has been replaced by *the answer lies with my personal set of beliefs*. There's no use in fighting it, for side-picking is a way of life.

So I'm down. Let's talk about good and evil. And let's talk about fat. It's a nutritional buzz at the moment – this "good fat" and "bad fat." Bad fats, of course, being easier to identify than an orangutan in an elevator – anything of the saturated and trans variety, or the collective menus of the fast food industry. And the good fats are coming out of the woodwork – omega 3s, monosaturateds, and avocado.

But I'm not talking about food. I'm talking about people.

As a skinny, I'm generally not supposed to comment on the "other side." It's seen as bad taste – kind of like white people rapping. But screw it; this honky is voyaging into the unknown. And the unknown is fat people.

Simply put, fat people are just like the rest of us. They have feelings, dreams, and ambitions, just more mass. And, like the general population (and given the trend in American lifestyle, they are soon to *be* the general population), they come in two forms: good and bad.

Yes, when it comes to fat people, there is good fat and bad fat. Or, as I like to refer to it, "happy fat" and "bitter fat."

Happy fat, of course, refers to the fat people we all love: Chris Farley (God rest his soul), John Goodman, most any black bassist, and the heavy girl from *Bridesmaids*. While obviously this is not an exhaustive list, it exemplifies the things we love in good fats – lightning wit, unbridled jolliness, and a generally sunny outlook on the world as a whole. Societally, we love happy/funny people, but we love happy/funny fat people even more. There's just something about an overweight human being that amplifies the positive qualities – maybe the fact that their smiles look bigger or they always seem comfortable in an easy chair or restaurant booth. Either way, we love the jolly fats for what they are: the roly-poly pandas of the human race. Fat people have a much higher comedic ceiling than equally funny skinny people – think Farley and John Belushi vs. Adam Sandler and Jimmy Fallon. See my point? It's no contest. Consequently, when funny fats lose the weight – and join the mundane ranks of the everyday comedian – it is a heartbreak on par with the day Princess Di died. Jonah Hill was once a solidly funny supporting fat actor, and now he is just an awkward, rectangular being with no real value to society. Same with a kid from my high school named Joe Winch. Used to be an adorable, round, rosy-cheeked boy, then he lost the weight, got a girlfriend, and began looking at the world with cynical eyes. It's just not the same. I'm glad your blood pressure has dropped and you're living a healthier lifestyle, but you no longer make me laugh. Can I interest you in some chicken wings?

Bitter fat, on the other hand, is the bane of our

QUITTING COLD STONE (AND OTHER STRUGGLES)

existence; it's almost as if Hitler had gone into the child pornography business. While I personally adore fat people – it is a state I am unable to achieve and am therefore jealous of – the human race as a whole tends to...um...look down upon obesity. So it's an uphill climb (if they can make it) from day one. And these bitter fats compound the negativity by being all pissed off about everything. I'm not going to name names here, but you know who I'm talking about; that kid in class who refuses to share his gum, that lady who hates Christmas out of spite, and the guy on the bus who intentionally takes up two seats. These people are incapable of humor or irony; they simply want to display their displeasure for the world in hopes that it infects others around them. They're just the worst. And this is the exact opposite of what they should be doing. The best course of action is clearly friendly diplomacy with the rest of the world. I mean, you're fat. At least be nice. As the great philosopher Chris Rock once laid out, "for every pound you are overweight, you gotta read another book, because you're gonna need to be way smarter than all those other motherfuckers." Or something like that – quoting Chris Rock is a slippery endeavor.

I'm not going to go as far as Chris and suggest habitual reading. But at least be cool. Be fun. *Be with us.* Say something moderately humorous, and add a sheepish smile afterwards; I guarantee it will make me – and most every intelligent person – love you. We *want* to love you; we want you to join the ranks of the jolly fat. Just give us a reason. Make me want to put my loving arm around you and proudly declare, "This is my fat friend."

Bitter fat, there is a better way. Consider the works of Farley, Belushi, et al, and be inspired. The grass really *is* greener on the other side. And don't worry, it tastes like Twinkies.

"HAPPY BIRTHDAY. HAVE A GREAT ONE!"

Formalities are an inevitable part of life. Nobody seems to like them, yet they persist. Work, social events, relationships – these are all formality-heavy undertakings and we've just seemed to accept this so as to not stir things up. Occasionally formalities even creep into leisure activities; they almost led me to abandon the game of golf – a game I thoroughly enjoy – at one point. Depending on who you're playing with, golf can be one of the most ceremonious activities known to man. Taking too long to hit, not taking long enough, hitting out of turn, wearing the wrong thing, not marking your ball on every green, accidentally stepping in someone's putting line, drinking 12 beers in nine holes – all these seemingly innocent gestures can make you look crass and unrefined in the eyes of "serious" golfers, i.e. people who actually enforce meaningless and fun-restricting rules during a casual round. These are the same guys who call hand-check fouls in pick-up basketball games. "Hey man," he'll say with a condescending tone on the seventh green, "did you just walk in my line? You know

QUITTING COLD STONE (AND OTHER STRUGGLES)

you're not supposed to walk in someone's line." *Oh I'm sorry, I thought this was a local municipal course, not the damn PGA Tour. I'll try to be more respectful of your line in the future. Nice pullover.*

The point is this: formalities suck. They are the things you're required to do to get to the enjoyable parts of life. I understand some things we cannot control, but some things we can. And I believe that when formalities invade the realm of Facebook – a largely user-created realm – it falls into the latter category.

Let's take a moment here to reflect on a time when Facebook was, essentially, awesome. Back in its heyday – the Golden Age, if you will – the 'Book was restricted only to those with a valid .edu email address. College students. It was a place to emote in any way you wanted, without repercussions. It was just for us – young stupid adults across the nation – and parental supervision was nonexistent. Your profile picture was most likely you passed out on someone's dorm room floor with a case of empty Keystone Light scattered throughout. Your "About Me" section probably said something about your ability to throw back whiskey shots like it was your job and 75% of your online interactions revolved around trying to identify and hook up with that cute brunette in your biology class. In short, it was a great time – the digital version of the free-love 60s. But then it exploded, Mark Zuckerburg grew fond of wiping his ass with $100 bills, and things slowly progressed south. High school students were allowed in and were soon followed by the aunts and grandmas. Potential employers began checking profiles for questionable behavior. All of a sudden we had to watch what we did and try to project a certain image. It became just like the real world, with a poke button. Nothing against aunts or grandmas – love you guys – but the dynamic certainly changed.

Ever since the Golden Age of Facebook, there's been an unspoken tradition of wishing someone a happy birthday via wall post. In the beginning, it was kind of cute –

Facebook reminded you whose birthday was that day, you sent them a little note (usually with reference to Natural Ice and/or beer-amids), and everyone went on their merry way. It wasn't an obligation, just an option. This has changed.

Over time, the birthday greetings have become an obligation. Someone will do it for one of their friends, and feel compelled to do it for the rest, even those to whom they have very little real acquaintance. Everyone else is writing on Laura Deehan's wall, and you for some reason feel bound to do the same. Nobody really knows why this ritual persists, yet we all perpetuate it. It's probably a combination of simple politeness and the old feeling of "I've always done this in the past, so why stop now?" And it's ridiculous.

In the Golden Age, you'd maybe have a few dozen birthday wall posts. Hopefully one from that cute brunette. Now there are hundreds; email inboxes are flooded with notifications, entire walls are seized and rendered useless for days, and every message seems to run together. Many of these are from people you don't even *know*, who clearly don't give a shit whether your birthday is happy or not, yet they fake it anyway. Even a lot of *actual* friends can't seem to formulate an original birthday wish anymore – at some point I suppose we all run out – and fall back on one of the go-to posts, which include but are not limited to:

"Happy birthday, have a great one!" "Hope it's an awesome day!" "Do something fun today!" "Hope you have an amazing birthday!" "It's been forever since I've seen you, we should hang out sometime!" (This is a lie; nobody involved wants to hang out. You probably only became Facebook friends with this person during that time it seemed necessary to add anyone you've ever heard of at any point in your life.) "Hope all is well!" "Have fun today!" And of course, "HAPPY BIRTHDAY!!!!" All caps and multiple exclamation points apparently make the comment more meaningful.

Of course there's nothing inherently wrong with any of this. After all, it is positivity, something our society seriously lacks at times, and who am I to tell good-intentioned well-wishers not to do their thing? If you want to wish your high school guidance counselor's niece's fiancé a happy birthday via Facebook, by all means use as many exclamation points as you'd like. Go nuts. I'm only saying that you shouldn't feel *obligated* to do this. Chances are if you are close enough to someone to warrant a happy birthday, you are also close enough to text them, call them, or (gasp!) tell them to their face. And if you do take one of these three avenues, you don't need to replicate the message on the 'Book for the whole world to see. I promise, it's cool. One is plenty. They get the idea.

Facebook birthday wishes will inevitably continue and in many cases they're actually warranted. Just please remember, like most things in life, this is a choice, not a requirement. There is no moral law indicating you have to do any of this, so use discretion, and I doubt anyone will even notice if you neglect your ex-boyfriend's college roommate's pot dealer on his special day. The world has enough formalities already.

THE ROAD TO BRANSON

Nightfall. Our bags were packed, and we wordlessly loaded up the Dodge Caravan. The excitement was palpable; the tingle of the open road and the uncertainty of the darkness. We were ready for our journey.

I was 11 years old, helping my father, two brothers, and cousin prepare the family vehicle. We slid open the side door and piled in suitcases and snack bags, and pillows for sleeping; it would be a long trip. As the final bag was situated, I saw the dim glow of headlights at the end of the driveway. My mother had been taking night classes for a master's degree and she was finally home. We greeted her and secured the home before firing up the van and all filing in. It was a tight fit between the luggage, but it would be worth it.

My dad put her in drive and we rumbled down our dirt road in the dark. We were finally on our way, headed south for a family vacation.

The destination? Branson, Missouri.

Yes, far from the beaches of Hawaii, sparkling waters of the Carribean or vineyards of California. That wasn't really our style. No, in those days my family was more about the cheap. My mom bought us bagged cereals and wouldn't let us use any soap that wasn't stolen from a hotel. There wasn't a whole lot of money to go around, so we necessarily did things as inexpensively as possible. Such as family vacations.

Honestly, the kids didn't even *know* that Branson wasn't a normal vacation destination at the time. We were either too young or brainwashed by our parents. I'm pretty sure they proposed the trip by coming home from work one day and asking, "Hey, you guys want to go to BRANSON (!!!) this summer!?!?!?!" I had no idea what Branson was, but how can an 11-year-old not get excited about a question posed in that way? We just didn't know any better; the parents spoke of theme parks and a hotel pool and restaurants(!!!). Being a frugal lot, eating out was a rare treat, so much that us kids were convinced Olive Garden and Chili's were international delicacies. A week in a foreign land (i.e. state) with MULTIPLE dinners out? I was visibly vibrating with excitement. My thoughts never even made it as far as the "Missouri" in "Branson, Missouri."

With the kids on board, the folks booked the trip, and in a few months we were driving down that dark road into the night, not even thinking about where we were actually going.

My parents had played us brilliantly. While we were all grateful to be going on a vacation – no matter the destination – they were making out like bandits. Not only were we headed to a place where the cost of living rivaled that of third world country, but they were hardly even paying for the damn hotel. That would be covered by the timeshare presentation they were attending.

You remember those? They might even still exist, the borderline scams that prey on people's desire to save money. Basically, some hospitality company offers a great deal on a hotel room or condo rental, provided you attend a "short informational session" about the fabulous timeshare options they offer. There's no obligation, they assure you, but they just want you to know about the tremendous opportunity that is available. It's the adult equivalent of giving college students a free sandwich or t-shirt for signing up for a credit card. It seems like a great deal, to get a few nights away at an insanely low price, only at the cost of an hour or so of your time.

Well as the saying goes, there's no such thing as a free hotel room, and the "brief presentation" you were promised is of course much longer and far more painful than you anticipated. Greasy real estate brokers drone on for hours about the "options that await," and you can't walk anywhere near your comped room without someone springing out of the shadows, eagerly shoving pamphlets in your face. It's all fairly exhausting. By the end of the ordeal, you probably wish you'd just paid full price for the damn thing.

Anyway, this was their plan. They were lured to Branson, Missouri, by a cheap hotel room and we were along for the ride.

Because of my mother's night school schedule, the only way the trip would work was if we left at 9 p.m. and drove through the night. No big deal, as the four boys could sleep the drive away in the spacious Dodge Caravan. Just two problems with that: as previously mentioned, the vehicle was packed full of suitcases and coolers and other general road trip/hotel stay equipment, thus rendering it considerably less roomy, and my parents required us to wear our seat belts the whole time. In the back seats. They obviously worried a little too much (translation: my mother worried too much and my father was required to agree with her) and did periodic random checks to make sure we were still buckled in. I tried explaining that we were so securely packed in between all the gear that we'd come out unscathed in any accident or rollover, and that it's quite uncomfortable to try to sleep in seatbelts, but the irrational mother love won out, as it always did. We stayed buckled.

QUITTING COLD STONE (AND OTHER STRUGGLES)

Somehow I managed to doze off while my father navigated the highways of southern Minnesota and Iowa. In the morning, we awoke from this pseudo sleep in the state of Missouri and stopped for a breakfast break in some park somewhere. There would be no restaurants yet; we still had food in the gigantic blue cooler, and thus spending money wasn't necessary. Breakfast was cheese, crackers, and summer sausage, because that's what we had.

I assumed we were close to our destination because we'd made it inside the proper state boundaries, but again was wrong. Have you ever looked at where Branson is on a map? Of course not. Why would you? But it's down there – very much in the *southern* part of Missouri, and damn near Arkansas. Since our traveling party had just recently crossed into the northern parts of Mizzou, we still had a healthy drive in front of us. I don't remember much of it, as I was probably listening to professional wrestling entrance music on my portable CD player (a thing I actually did) or fighting with my cousin Julian.

I should probably explain the Julian thing, as he was a central figure in our lives in those days. Julian was a year younger than me, from San Francisco, and a straight 50/50 split of Korean and American. Every summer in my adolescence, he would travel to Minnesota and stay with my family for a month or two – living at our house, attending our social functions, and just generally being a part of our clan. Looking back, I'm not actually sure why this was; it's like my folks had some sort of custody timeshare with his parents or something. He was an only child, so maybe my uncle (his father) thought it would be a good way to assimilate him to the ways of boys his age. Hell, maybe they just wanted a break from the little bastard. Whatever the reason, my parents always seemed happy to take him off their hands for a few months in the summer. So each June, Julian walked off a plane with a single suitcase and proceeded to wear the same three t-shirts for the next seven weeks. Life was simpler back then.

Naturally, my brothers and I fought with him constantly. Despite being family, he was a foreigner in our land, and his attitude was a little different than ours on a lot of things. For one, he was kind of a little shit. And not to toot my own horn or anything, but the three Neumann boys were pretty much exemplary citizens; we stayed out of trouble, did our chores on time, and parted our hair to the side. Three squeaky clean, rosy cheeked youngsters from stand-up parents. Julian, on the other hand, had an attitude about everything. He talked back to my parents and acted as if the things we did were beneath him.

Case in point: food. One Christmas Eve he (allegedly) forced himself to throw up at the dinner table simply in protest of the menu. Another time, the family was seated around the dinner table, chowing down on hamburgers Dad had made on the grill. Julian was tearing into his just like the rest of us, until halfway through his eyes narrowed in an accusatory nature, and he slowly lowered the burger to his plate.

"Donna," he asked my mother calmly, "where did this beef come from?"

"Um, the grocery store," she answered, confused.

"*Which* grocery store?"

"Uhhhh...Brinks Market. Why?"

His eyes narrowed further. "Do they grind their own meat?"

"I don't know," she answered honestly. "Probably not."

Julian let out an audible groan and pushed the plate away from him. "Gross." he said. "I'm not eating it."

We never really figured out what the fuck that was all about.

Eventually Julian grew up to be an upstanding young man. But in those days, he was a poor-mannered snot nosed kid in a faded Chicago Bulls t-shirt. My parents used their time with him as an opportunity to work on those manners, and try to get him to come around to a respectable method of human interaction. They put constant emphasis on using the word "please" – a concept that had been beaten into the Neumann boys early on but was foreign to Julian – and strictly outlawed the use of "shut up;" it was simply referred to as the "forbidden word."

Julian was slow to warm to the new rules. "Please" was a daily struggle, and he found a workaround for the "shut up" rule – instead of explicitly telling me to shut up, he would just tell me to "forbidden word" instead. For example:

Sam: "Julian, hurry up and get in the car. We gotta go."
Julian: "Forbidden word, Sam."

I must admit, it had pretty much the same effect. The kid had a way of beating the system.

We rambled south through Missouri as the kids threw things at each other and the parents continually told us to stop. After a long day of travel and infighting, we began to see the signs for Branson. We were near.

The billboards gave the first indications of the odd cultural mishmash that Branson was – or, more accurately, was trying to be. From what I could gather, Branson was equal parts western horse ranch, Las Vegas show, and Super 8 Motel. Huge illuminated signs lined the highway, advertising horseback riding, magic shows, cheap lodging, and most of all, showgirls. Billboards for showgirls and burlesque events were everywhere, each claiming to be the best in town. Middle aged women in scant sparkly outfits stared down at us and demanded we come see their "once in a lifetime" show, giving me that awkward feeling of knowing my parents and I were both looking at the same, questionably explicit picture. I honestly couldn't even tell if the shows were supposed to be pornographic; it didn't really seem like it – more like they were advertising good old-fashioned synchronized dancing over martinis – but then I'm not really sure what the draw was. No matter, it was obvious we wouldn't be attending any of these shows, even if they were the best in town.

As we arrived in the darkness, it was immediately obvious that Branson was an embodiment of the tacky tourist trap. It smelled of cigarettes and small bills and seemed to have a Best Western or La Quinta Inn on each block. It was an overgrown town, not a city, and you didn't get the idea that anyone really cared.

And honestly, neither did we; the Neumann troupe wasn't some snotty club of high society, but a hardworking, salt of the earth collection of Midwestern folk. We didn't need the *real* Las Vegas when Branson was pretty much a cheaper version of the same thing, albeit smaller, partially deserted, and lacking gambling or attractive people. Seriously though, we were happy – we had a hotel (probably with a POOL!) and restaurants. That pretty much made any place heaven.

The first night was low key – checking into the hotel (one room for six of us), getting situated, and watching cable television, to which we were not privy at home. I think dinner was some leftover sandwiches from the ride. We all turned in fairly early, for my parents had an important timeshare presentation in the morning.

The folks left just before eight to go pay the piper. They told us they just had a short meeting, and they'd be back no later than ten. We were to occupy ourselves until then.

The kids spent most of the morning watching SportsCenter, eating Twizzlers, and performing pro wrestling moves on one another, using the beds as crash pads. When eleven o'clock rolled around and we still hadn't heard from the 'rents, we started to wonder – cabin fever was setting in. There wasn't a whole lot to do other than watch TV, and we were starting to realize that the shows on cable weren't really any better than those on normal TV. Also, the tap water tasted strongly of chlorine. This was a concern. But there wasn't much we could do, for we were specifically instructed not to leave the room under any circumstances (the whole mom/worry thing). So we carried on and waited.

Noon came and we were restless. Still no word from the parents, I began to entertain the idea that they might've driven to southern Missouri just to abandon us in a nondescript hotel room. With three adolescent boys and an unruly nephew from out of state, I wouldn't have blamed them. I pictured the two of them speeding down the highway in the Caravan, my father with his foot on the gas and mom in the front seat yelling "WOOOO!" and taking pulls straight from a bottle of whiskey. In this imagination, they were happy.

Finally they barged back into the room damn near one o'clock. Their eyes were tired, their brains clearly fried, and it seemed the "short presentation" turned out to be quite an ordeal.

"That was *awful*," my dad said as he plopped down on one of the beds. "Four and a half hours of people constantly trying to sell you something."

"Did you buy anything?" I asked. I knew the answer.

"No! We told them up front we weren't gonna buy anything. And still..." his eyes drifted, "four and a half hours..."

They'd clearly underestimated the wrath of the timeshare presentation. Both Mom and Dad probably just wanted to sit down and relax, but unfortunately for them, there was no rest for the weary; we were ready to have some damn fun.

And over the next few days, we did have fun. Honestly too much to list fully here, so to avoid this becoming a book of its own, I'll hit the bullet points. We:

- Went to Silver Dollar City, this seriously badass lumberjack inspired amusement park. I love rides, and this place had good ones; not just tilt-a-whirls and Ferris wheels, we're talking high speed rails and ball-shrinking free-falls. The first ride we did was a roller coaster that topped out at 50 mph, which turned my younger brother into a blubbering mess by the first twist in the track. He cried the entire ride, with the rest of us trying to ignore him and enjoy ourselves. We probably should've provided a little more support, considering he was like seven at the time, but whatever.

Emotional episodes aside, the day was a smashing success, with thrill rides, funnel cakes, and overpriced colas. The only small downer was my dad threatening to call the day off altogether when he found out he'd have to pay $50 a head to get in. I don't blame him – that's kind of outlandish, especially in those days – but we lobbied hard enough to break him down and secure the tickets. It was that or a family burlesque show, after all.

- Used the hotel pool. It was just a normal hotel, and thus a normal pool, but much like eating out, pools were a rare treat in our family. I splashed away until my hands were pruned.

- Went to restaurants. More than once. Fuck. Yes. It was divine. The one that sticks out in memory was a legitimate, non-chain steakhouse with an open kitchen setup. Only a few large sheets of Plexiglas separated the clientele from the kitchen staff, and us boys wandered over and gazed through the glass at the cooks grilling those delicious hunks of meat. A few times they even acknowledged us by squirting water at the Plexiglas where we were standing. It was all great fun, and I think we talked about it for a few years.

- Also ate in our hotel room. This was expected. Being on vacation for the better part of a week, it wasn't like we were going to eat *all* of our meals out. This gave my mother a chance to experiment with her impressive frugality, and make decent-tasting meals for the whole family out of a simple $20 grocery store run. She made solid sub sandwiches with cheap Oscar Meyer meats and generic cheeses, and satisfied our need for sweetness and adventure with Sam's Choice sodas and peanut M&Ms. It wasn't as good as Applebee's, but it was more than passable.

And on the way home, with the fun and games over, my parents sick of the four boys and the four boys sick of each other, what little money we had was nearly dried up. My father explained we had enough for gas and one small meal for the last part of the drive. There were no credit cards – at least none used by my parents – in those days. On the last leg of the journey back, probably somewhere in Iowa, we pulled into a McDonald's drive-thru. McDonald's wasn't a frequent spot for my family to eat, but quite honestly it was the cheapest option.

"Now remember," my dad said, "you can each have something *small*, like a cheeseburger. No meal deals or anything like that. We have water to drink."

We all nodded in understanding, and then went down the line with our orders.

"I'll have a hamburger," my older brother said.

"Same for me," was my order.

"I'll have a hamburger too," said the littlest Neumann. It was Julian's turn.

He glanced at the menu. "Um, I'll have a number two." He was asking for a meal.

My dad sighed from the driver's seat. "Julian..."

"Oh, sorry." Julian said, realizing his error. "I'll have a number two, *please.*"

We got four hamburgers and drove away.

DEAR PARKING SERVICES

Dear Parking Services,

Hello. My name is Sam. In fact, we've met before; I was the one on the phone with you just a minute ago. Since I wasn't articulating my feelings that well, I thought I'd write you, just to clear the air.

You see, I don't hate you. I just want to know why you are the way you are – the exterminator of good times, the crusader against happiness, the perpetuator of technicality. I don't question your duty. Keeping parking lots free of unlawful parkers and other miscreants is of utmost priority, and I'm well aware that I *was* parked illegally. But why must you go to the extreme with your occupation? You've clearly found that writing parking tickets is your calling in life, and for that I applaud you, but the fervent nature in which you execute said calling is slightly baffling to me. For instance, was it really necessary to give me three consecutive tickets for the same parking violation? Wouldn't one, or even two have sufficed? I gladly would've paid two, since I am a good American who understands commerce and likes to make a deal. But sadly, your policies were without leeway. Very well, three it is.

QUITTING COLD STONE (AND OTHER STRUGGLES)

But why the excess of pictures taken? I understand you need photo evidence, so as to safeguard against disgruntled offenders who think they can talk their way out of these things – which, believe me, I would've tried, so props to you – but were 10 photos really called for? I admit, despite my car's age, I do keep it looking good, so I can see how you might want to admire it later from the comfort of your own home, but I assure you three or four pictures would've done the trick.

And finally, let's discuss the late fee. This one really befuddles a common man like myself. Bear with me; since the vehicle in question was parked behind a locked chain-linked fence (which would seem like a place out-of-the-way and obsolete enough not to cause trouble, and that was really my intent, but I digress), you were not able to reach the car and serve the tickets on its windshield, in traditional parking cadet fashion. Instead, you mailed them, and let me first just say I appreciate your support of the United States Postal Service. They're really hurting right now, so your patriotism is admirable. But then, dear parking people, the citations did not reach me until after the arbitrary and much-sooner-than-reasonable deadline for payment, and thus you asked for a late fee. This seems odd, for a small-minded Midwesterner like myself cannot know to pay a citation before I am notified that the citation exists, but my arguments to that point didn't seem to resonate with you. Those are the rules, I was told, and the rules are rigid.

I would fight you on this, but the excess of photographic proof and diligent note taking done by your office would make that an exercise in futility; plus I'm not much of a fighter anyway. Instead, I just want to say I'm sorry. I'm sorry, parking people, that life has been so unkind to you. Clearly you've been beaten down and pushed in the proverbial mud since childhood, for that is the only logical scenario that would breed a creature so bitter and intent on others' unhappiness that they would actually willfully work for a branch of government of with the sole purpose of ruining people's days. It must be very tough for you.

In high school you were the fat kid with acne, and you spent most of your days trying to stop your peers from bombarding you with corn nuts and other small projectiles in the hallways. This, for some reason, you were unable to get past as you matured, and now your mission each morning is to *get back at those bastards for what they've done*. I would tell you that, at 30 years of age or so, it's time to forgive and move on, but I don't think it would do much good. Or perhaps you were a goth, with the black clothes and dog collars and face paint and Manson shirts, and while the wardrobe is gone, the attitude on life inexplicably remains. If that is the case, go ahead and keep writing parking tickets, but please stop performing sacrifices on your neighbors' cats, okay? Or maybe you're just a person with a natural inclination towards bitterness and power trips, but you failed out of the police academy. In that scenario, I'd suggest you just go and die somewhere.

Okay, I'm not serious about the dying part. That seems a little extreme, and extremity is the very thing I'm speaking out against, isn't it? But something must be done, and since the overwhelming amount of evidence you've compiled prohibits me from contesting the parking tickets, I'll just have to fuck up your world instead. Yes, miserable loner, I have a plan. I'm not going to hurt you, but I'd like you to feel a similar level of irritation as I did when dealing with you. So I'm going to break into your place of residence one night. You'll be sleeping, probably on the couch with an empty bag of Doritos on your chest, with the TV left on. This is fine – I work quietly, so I won't wake you. My first order of business is finding your collection of Star Wars figurines and cutting the limbs off each of them. I know how much they mean to you and I feel this is a good place to start the sabotage. After that, I will locate your Xbox Live headset and piss on it. This way, the next time you're pwning noobs on Call of Duty in an online skirmish, you will smell my urine. I might even eat some asparagus first just to amplify things. Finally, I will enter your room and draw mustaches on all of your Jonathan Taylor Thomas posters. It's kind of weird that you like him so much, especially at your age (and, you know...you're a guy. And Home Improvement was like 20 years ago), but any defamation of J.T.T. will surely bring you to your knees. This, I'm afraid to say, will bring a smile to my face.

After I exit, I plan on finding your car in the driveway and attaching the boot I bought off Craigslist to one of the tires. Then, and only then, you will finally understand: that kinda sucks, doesn't it?

DEFENDING NICKELBACK

Okay, everyone relax. Calm down, please. Take a deep breath, close your eyes, count to ten, and resist the urge to send me an envelope full of anthrax. Hold off on the "REALLY Sam?!?!" and "I didn't think even you would stoop this low" comments. Put on some red lipstick, cross me off your "People to Kill" list – at least temporarily – and just give me a chance to explain myself.

I can't fault you for having these snap reactions – with a title like "Defending Nickelback," a certain amount of anger is unavoidable from the majority of people before they've even read the first line. It's only natural. Saying anything remotely positive about this categorically soulless band is almost akin to arguing, "You know, Osama Bin Laden wasn't actually *that* bad a guy." No red blooded American will have it, and for good reason. When I told my younger brother I was considering writing this entry, he likened Nickelback to O.J. Simpson. I told him I didn't follow.

"O.J. was good," he said, "then he killed people. Nickelback was good; then they killed music."

Fair point, and it leads me to my thesis:

QUITTING COLD STONE (AND OTHER STRUGGLES)

Nickelback's first major-label release, *The State*, is a pretty good rock album. Was then, is now.

I understand this might be hard to believe, even impossible for someone who only knows the band as they are today: an insanely commercial, label-controlled monstrosity that sticks to a rigorous (and all-around terrible) formula designed to churn out a large volume of product that has the singular goal of *selling*. It's true; modern-day Nickelback represents everything that's wrong with the music industry and popular music in general. They make a ton of money for consistently putting out a rudimentary, unimaginative, and kind of awful product. They must have fans – like millions upon millions, as total album sales for the band are currently hovering around 35 million – yet nobody seems to know one. It's sort of like Sarah Palin supporters – clearly they exist, but I can't remember the last person to whom I've spoken that openly admitted to it. Regardless of how wacky or mainstream any of my friends' musical tastes might be, they are all quick to tell anyone who will listen how much they despise Nickelback. And it's not just close friends – this pretty much extends to every casual acquaintance. Nearly everyone I've ever met seems uniformly offended by this band.

We all hate Nickelback for what they are today: low-level commercial pop rock. But it wasn't always that way.

There was a time near the turn of the century (and millennium) when 13 year-old Sam was in love with "rock." I was, as memory serves, struggling with my own identity – stuck in an odd purgatory between video gaming and skateboarding – and trying desperately to stay out of the nerd category at school. I also remember hating 70% of the kids my age for one reason or another. It's the sinister paradox I assume of adolescence; despise your peers but seek their approval at the same time. Anyway, "rock" seemed to be the remedy for all of this – loud and edgy enough to make me feel at least semi-cool, and just *slightly* off the beaten path so as not to make me feel like a conformist. At the time, rap was infiltrating the mainstream pop charts and all the boys and girls at Chisago Lakes Middle School were gradually deciding it was the only thing to which they wanted to listen. Seemingly out of nowhere, rap was suddenly cool. The release of Dr. Dre's *2001* brought this to a crescendo as Caucasians around the country monotonously sung the closing lines of *The Next Episode* until the cows came home. It was nearly as obnoxious as the way white trash housewives belt out the lyrics to *Don't Stop Believing* every Saturday night. Rap was *in* in suburbia and the hill country, and from what I can tell it was the first time in history that white kids wished they were black.

Being the little contrarian bastard I was (and to some extent still am), I was having none of this. I did not want to be a white kid that wanted to be black; I was comfortable in my Caucasionality (a word I just made up), so I began listening to thrash metal and attending white pride rallies. Kidding, of course, but I did adopt modern rock and roll as my personal soundtrack. It was the perfect drug – I was running the opposite way of this fleeting rap obsession and I damn sure wasn't jumping on the Journey train, so straightforward, no bullshit rock was the only popular genre left. Because country sucks.

I felt like I *should* commit to loud, semi-dark modern rock, and for a while I actually did. I listened to the radio stations, I read the magazines, I bought the CDs and hid them from my parents. Never did something strike as much fear in people in their forties as that little black and white warning in the bottom corner of disc cases, and conversely the "parental advisory" became a badge of honor for America's youth. I listened to a lot of shitty bands back then (Staind, Disturbed, Limp Bizkit, and Godsmack to name a handful), but during this same time I also found some legitimately solid works of rock and roll – most notably Incubus' *Make Yourself,* and yes, Nickelback's *The State*.

Nickelback did a few indie label albums before

QUITTING COLD STONE (AND OTHER STRUGGLES)

The State, which I and most every person have never heard. When they released *The State* in 2000, popular rock had made the slow transition out of grunge and was moving into whatever the hell it is currently, and this album was one of the few that adequately bridged the gap. It was clean but not overproduced, abrasive but not muddy, and the lyrics were interesting without being overthought. Quite simply, the record was solid – if unspectacular – classic rock adapted to the 21st century. Nothing about it was overstated (a fundamental contrast to modern-day Nickelback), and every single track felt, for lack of a better term, *real*.

I believe that's because, from what I gather, at the time the band *was* real. They had never had a major label release, which means they probably had very little money, they devoted most of their time to playing live music and consuming chemicals, which means they understood what rock and roll was about, and they were from Canada, so it's unlikely many people took them seriously. Nickelback was a glorified garage band at this point, and having experienced such little commercial success granted them the luxury of ignorance – they hadn't yet been exposed to so many of the factors that ultimately led to the band turning to complete shit: producers, label reps, constant spotlight, industry parties, and the mainstream formula for successful songwriting. In short, a taste of the big time. It is a blissful innocence every band has at some point before they hit it big, and I suspect it's also the reason most bands do their best work early on. The mindset of a young artist with the only goal of creating great music is probably the single most important aspect of turning out a good product, and it only exists until The Man shows up and starts to chip away at it. Once you learn certain things, you can't unlearn them. As soon as a band signs with a label and begins getting market and branding advice, that 21 year-old with a guitar in his hands and a song in his heart is no longer just that – he is now a businessman. And in musical terms, there's nothing more stifling to creativity than capitalism.

The test, of course, of how much these newfound factors ruin a group's creative makeup is based purely on how each individual handles them. And Nickelback handled them terribly. Never in my short time as a music fan have I seen a band of any value so willingly "take the money and run." With the release of their next album, *Silver Side Up*, the single "How You Remind Me" instantly became a smash hit – practically played across the board on every contemporary radio station – and the cash registers began ringing. Nearly everything they recorded from here on out followed the formula of this one song, tossing aside their earlier sound completely and neglecting to revisit it ever again. Whatever integrity Nickelback had as a rock band, they were far too eager to waive it all for a few zeros on the end of those paychecks. Years later the band released another smash hit (one of many) entitled "Rockstar," with frontman Chad Kroeger repeatedly proclaiming:

I'm gonna trade this life for fortune and fame / I'd even cut my hair and change my name.

It was an autobiography. Literally he did neither, but metaphorically he shaved his head and went by Emanuel Bard. Just tell me what you want and I'll give it to you, as long as the money and the women and the drugs and the TRL spots keep coming.

A prototypical sellout, and it's a damn shame. Now, it's hard for me to *completely* condemn any person for taking the money, for though we all assume we'd take the noble path, none of us actually know how we'd respond until faced with the same situation. But that's an argument for a different time – the point is, the metamorphosis is complete for Nickelback, and it's impossible to ever go back. But I don't think that discredits anything of worth the band might've done in the past. And I think *The State* falls into that category. I still get chills when the distortion ramps up on "Leader of Men" (the lead single), and even as I listen to the album now and try to dislike it due to the subsequent wrongs the band has done the musical industry, I can't. I suppose it's possible it's just a youthful nostalgia I'm feeling, but I don't think that's it; I've pretty much written off most other bands I listened to at the time. I can listen to the record all the way through without getting bored or annoyed, and I honestly think that's pretty rare.

Of course, I don't expect you to trust me on this, and at this point there's really no way to convince someone what I'm saying is true. I'd love to just tell you to listen to the album, then sit back with arms folded and a smug grin as the undeniable sonic goodness of the songs won you over. But this is impossible – the bias is too deep by now. Even if the music is actually solid, no-bullshit rock and roll, what a contemporary music fan knows about Nickelback now and the scars of so many musical wrongs they've likely come to associate with Chad Kroeger's voice would cloud their sense of perspective. It's just the natural progression. Even if I sat someone down and played Pink Floyd's *Dark Side of the Moon*, if I was somehow able to convince them that it was written and recorded by Nickelback, they'd tell me it was mass-produced garbage. And this is okay; we all get a little gun-shy after so many terrible songs are forced upon us by one group. Just another label-controlled monstrosity selling millions of records without producing anything of real consequence or value. No big deal.

But at least for one band, it wasn't always that way.

MOTHER NATURE IS A TRAMP

"Oh you didn't hear? I-76 is closed, honey."

The woman told me this from behind the counter with a look of half pity and half surprise that I hadn't yet heard the big news. It was 7 a.m. on a Friday and I was standing in a Shell station somewhere east of Denver, just wanting to pay for my beef jerky and get on my way without incident.

"Yeah," she continued, "it's closed from Sterling to Nebraska. Probably because of that snowstorm they got last night."

I thanked her and exited the store. I had no knowledge of a snowstorm – didn't think to check for such things in the middle of April – nor did I have any idea where Sterling was, though I correctly assumed it was somewhere between my current location and my destination. I got in my car and looked at a map, checked for alternate routes, found nothing, and turned back on the freeway. There was no reason to alter my plans at this point.

One spring weekend, I decided to head back to Ames, Iowa, for Veishea, Iowa State's annual booze-soaked spring celebration of everything that is good. I like Veishea

QUITTING COLD STONE (AND OTHER STRUGGLES)

enough to make a 10-hour drive, mostly across Nebraska, seem like a good idea, plus most of the college gang would be back and it had been far too long since I'd seen them. I had been looking forward to this weekend for quite some time. This gas station woman's ominous yet ambiguous warnings about snowstorms and closed interstates did little to temper my enthusiasm – she was most likely flat wrong or on meth, possibly both. Regardless, she couldn't be trusted. I turned up the stereo and pressed on.

Roughly an hour of easterly driving later, I found out that Sterling, Colorado, did indeed exist and Interstate 76 was in fact closed from it to Nebraska. The gigantic orange highway signs told me as much as they demanded I exit the freeway immediately. Rather pushy, those signs. Whoever decided to close the freeway wasn't all that accommodating either; they didn't think it necessary to provide us a detour or anything, instead just funneling all of the wayward travelers down the off-ramp and into the parking lot of a large but over-inhabited truck stop. There wasn't a whole lot else going on in Sterling. Seeing no other real option, I parked and headed into the establishment, hoping to pick up some more information on what the hell was going on. I didn't even see any snow.

Once inside I used the bathroom and then casually slipped into a circle of stranded Hispanic truck drivers, hoping I wouldn't look out of place. They spoke Spanish to each other for a minute or so, then kindly translated the conversation for me and another white face that had joined the group. The rundown was this: bad storm near the Nebraska border the previous night, something like a foot of snow and glare ice in places, the road would be opened at 10 a.m. at the earliest. That was in two hours. The apparent group leader spoke of a tangled web of back roads that could conceivably skirt the freeway and take you through to Nebraska, where you'd meet up with Interstate 80, presumably in working order.

"So you think Highway 6 is the best way to go?" I asked

him.

He shrugged and smiled. "Not sure. No way of knowing, really."

I thanked the panel and returned to my car, where I opened the trunk and dug out a massive United States atlas that has been back there for years. Thank you Uncle Brian, you did say it would come in handy at some point. Turning to Colorado/Nebraska, I plotted my route – there was no way in hell I was hanging around this forsaken rock for two hours just for the *possibility* of the road opening. I found a few highways that looked – as far as you can tell from an atlas – fairly major and not too far out of the way, and my path was set. I would take 6 east, then 23 northeast until I hit highway 61, which would take me north into Nebraska and meet up with I-80. As soon as I was on 80, I'd set the cruise at 85 and make up for lost time. This would work.

The trek began fairly well – mostly clear roads and a consistent speed between 60 and 65, which I considered a win since I was stuck behind six or seven other vehicles. Our ragtag caravan rolled through a few eastern Colorado farming towns, each of which were essentially one gas station and a grain elevator. As we ventured farther across the countryside, I finally found the snow, and it deepened with every mile. The sky was perfectly clear and things were beginning to melt, but soon the wind picked up and made the going a little slower. Then a lot slower. I was down around 35 mph, and getting impatient.

Finally I arrived in Holyoke, Colorado, where I could get on Highway 23 and split from this funeral procession. I did, and it was initially glorious – nothing but the open road in front of me and the whole damn world as my oyster, by God! Unfortunately the road conditions here were far worse; the wind was whipping now, blowing the snow across the road with fury and creating some seriously dangerous patches of covered pavement. I never lost control across one of these areas, but it did make me reduce my speed below 30 mph, and I cringed at the thought of lost time. As the road rambled on, it became clear that it wasn't meant for mass transit. It seemed the only ones using this path were myself and semi-trucks, and each time one would pass me, it created a gust of wind that nearly knocked my car off the road, not to mention spray an avalanche of half-melted snow on my windshield. I audibly cursed each one every time this happened, as if they were attempting to cover me in snow and murder me. I even openly gave a few the finger, which somehow made me feel a little better.

When I crossed the Nebraska border I saw nothing but more high winds, snow-covered road, and grain elevators. Just the fact that I was in that state made everything seem worse. Eventually I made it to the "town" of Grant, where I turned north onto the last leg of my detour and dreamed of the open, dry freeway that awaited. The road here was even worse –the snow covered most of it – so maintaining the perfect speed was crucial; too fast and I'd spin out and surely die, too slow and I'd likely get my car stuck in a drift. I'd estimate this was somewhere near 27 mph. It was true white-knuckle shit. There were no semis navigating this road (this part was too dangerous even for professional drivers, evidently), only beat up pickup trucks driven by local farmers, each of whom shot me a sympathetic glance and gave me the two-finger wave as they passed. Sometimes I waved back, but mostly I just concentrated.

Miraculously I made it to the town of Ogallala, which was where the road met I-80, my theoretical deliverance from this mess. I was so excited I almost pissed my pants, though that could've been the result of 24 ounces of coffee and my comically small bladder. Either way, I was happy. But as I approached the on-ramp for I-80 east, my heart sank at what I saw – a line of cars parked along the shoulder. I wasn't sure what this meant, I only knew it wasn't good. Sure enough, as I got close enough to the ramp, I saw the ominous steel gate closed with DO NOT ENTER adorning the face. This freeway was also closed. It was 10 a.m.

Another truck stop, another piss break, another conversation with local employees and stranded travelers. Also one extremely dissatisfying 6-inch Subway sandwich. Word had it the road was nearly clear of snow, but officials needed to tend to a number of semi-truck accidents to the east before they could open it up again. These accidents had happened the previous night when, as legend had it, freezing rain turned the pavement into an ice rink. Some of the weary travelers had been stranded since then. They spoke of total carnage. I hated everything.

I sat in the truck stop for as long as I could stomach before buying more snacks to occupy my time and heading back out to my car. There I plopped down in the driver seat, parked and watched the freeway for movement, just as most of the others in the lot were doing. I-80 West was also currently closed, and I sure as hell wasn't retracing my tracks across podunk Nebraska, so there was literally nowhere for me to go. I began texting friends and telling them I might not make it; every minute that passed was making a long trip even longer, and I could only realistically wait so long before the whole thing became impractical. An hour passed and the officials appeared to reopen 80 West – at least now my escape route was an option. I could be home in three hours in decent conditions. I put on an audio book and tilted my seat back as I watched the clock, making arbitrary deadlines and breaking them. *If the road isn't opened by noon,* I'd say to myself, *I'm turning back.* But noon came and I did nothing. I was really looking forward to the weekend and not yet willing to give up, so I simply sat there. Three hours I waited in all, until finally I couldn't take it any longer. I started the engine and began driving – the new plan was to take a narrow frontage road east to the next possible freeway exit. If the eastbound ramp was open, I'd take it. If not, I'd turn back, for real this time.

Twenty minutes later I reached I-80 yet again, and as it approached I for some reason became nervous. There was absolutely nobody around, and this felt vaguely illegal. No matter, my decision was made. My car came to the eastbound ramp, and miraculously it was wide open. Glory! I paused, looked around, and continued onto the freeway. What I found was a completely clear and sun-dried road, devoid of semi wrecks or travelers of any kind. I was completely alone. I smiled, increased my speed to 95, and called a friend to tell him to expect me in seven hours.

Mother Nature, I've beaten you again. Why must we fight like this?

TO THE GUY WHO LEAVES HIS GROCERY CART IN THE MIDDLE OF THE PARKING LOT

I understand your plight; it is, after all, a rough world out there. Political discourse is depressing, the kids' tuition just keeps going up, and no matter how hard you wish her back, Whitney Houston is still gone. Things are tough for all of us, but you seem to be taking it especially hard. This is evident by the fact that you're unable to complete simple human tasks, like returning your grocery cart to the conveniently-placed cart corral merely feet away from your vehicle after you're done shopping. Instead, you load your stuff into your trunk, then before hopping in the driver seat to leave, you give the cart a gentle shove away from you, sending it sailing into some inconvenient region of the parking lot (and probably someone else's car). Your indifference to the matter is striking. The cart inevitably comes to a rest in the shared corners of four separate spots, making it impractical for anyone else to park in any of them.

If you need someone to talk to, or even a shoulder to

QUITTING COLD STONE (AND OTHER STRUGGLES)

cry on, I am here for you. Unfortunately you drove off pretty fast, so we'll probably never get that chance. Instead, I'm going to try to justify your behavior, for surely there is a reason you do what you do. Perhaps this will calm down the rest of the shoppers/humanity, who all seem to be pretty irritated with you. And rightfully so, because, hey, you kind of look like a dick.

Option 1: You are extremely busy.

Yes, being the titan of trade, captain of industry, or all-around badass businessman/woman you are, you certainly don't have time for a superfluous task in the name of common courtesy. You are far too busy. The rest of us, we have a social obligation to move our carts out of the way, and to round them up in a convenient location for the grocery store employees. We lowly serfs need to do this because we haven't reached your status in life, and thus haven't earned your exemption from adult responsibility. Plus, we want to spend as much time in that parking lot as possible, in order to delay returning to our pathetic and depressing lives as long as we can. If we were important, like you clearly are, maybe we could justify leaving the carts wherever we wanted, thereby inconveniencing everyone else. But alas, we are not. *Sigh.*

But you, sir, go ahead and leave that cart wherever you damn well please. You've earned it. You're too busy to be bothered with such a banal task anyway, and surely one of the common folk will take care of it for you, just as they do in every other area of life. And go ahead and flick your cigarette butt out your window; we'll take care of that, too. You are one of the chosen people, and I'm sure it's what God would want.

Option 2: You are extremely lazy.

Like a deadbeat roommate drooling on the couch at three in the afternoon, you are a lazy sack of shit. You are uninterested in hard work or delayed gratification; instead, your mind is consistently consumed with what will make you feel good *right now*. And of course, selfless acts of kindness are not immediately gratifying (at least not as gratifying as fried mozzarella sticks and ranch dressing, am I right?), so why take part in them? You don't owe the world anything. You don't see these other shoppers helping *you* out when you've been sitting on the couch for 10 straight hours and the remote is out of reach, now do you? They were not there for you in your time of need, so why should you be there for them?

And even if you did want to help out and do your part as a human being...that's, like, a lot of work. How can they expect you to go the extra mile for people you don't even know? Surely the grocery store has people on staff to clean up after the customers, anyway. Speaking of which, I wonder if any of them would be willing to push you around in your cart while you do your shopping next time. Those aisles are awfully long, after all.

Option 3: You are a moron.

It's not your fault, really; it's just that returning a grocery cart to where it's supposed to go is really *hard* for you. You're not a bad person, you're just an idiot. Even the simplest tasks, like reading bus maps or shaving without cutting yourself or, I don't know, returning a shopping cart to an area clearly marked "RETURN CARTS HERE"...these things cause you massive confusion (or is it confusement? Words are hard). Really, it's best for you to focus on getting through the day in one piece rather than try to go the extra few feet. Even if you wanted to return your cart properly, chances are you wouldn't know how to do it.

You have special needs and probably get monthly checks from the government. Somehow, they still let you drive, which is what got us in this mess in the first place (people who walk to the grocery store rarely buy enough to necessitate a cart). May God help the other drivers on your way home. Remember, 10 and 2, eyes on the road, and check your blind spot. Don't worry about the cart – I'll get it.

In Conclusion.

So which one are you, assface? Which option is the truth?

I'm not sure. But I'd venture a guess that you probably think you're Option 1, when in reality it's a combination of Options 2 and 3. You are not too busy to put your cart away. The damn Sultan of Agrabah isn't too busy for 30 seconds worth of uniform kindness.

No, it's much more likely you are just a lazy dumbass. You probably wear hats sideways, drink Monster energy drinks, keep one ear pierced after the age of 40, own lots of snowmobile jackets, and/or do a host of similar things that are a dead giveaway of your kind. You might even work in parking meter enforcement. You contribute little of value to society, and wherever you go, everyone kind of wishes you weren't there.

Asswipe, there isn't much going for you. So why not make it at least one redeeming quality, extend some common courtesy, and put your damn cart away? Trust me, you have the time.

ALL OVERRATED LIST, PART 1

Often when we talk of bands or sports teams, we like to tag them with "overrated" or "underrated" when the public perception of one of them differs from our own. Personally, I like to apply this system to people and everyday items as well, and that's what this entry is about.

Basically, we're just here to discuss any public figure – music, sports, TV, etc. – that is generally thought of as more or less valuable than they actually are. It'll be broken up into two parts, and I'll of course start with the overrated list, because I am a dick.

Before we get started, keep in mind that calling someone overrated doesn't mean I think they have no value, just that I think the public perception of them is unwarrantedly rosy. And I will not include any pop R&B singers – such as Bruno Mars or something called Trey Songz – for you can just assume I think they all suck. Anyway, in no particular order...

Tyler Perry
You may know him from *Tyler Perry's House of Pain*, *Meet the Browns*, the film *Diary of a Mad Black Woman*,

and countless other painfully unfunny TBS programs that you probably haven't seen either. He is a writer/director/producer who allegedly makes comedies, though I don't believe there is documented proof of a sane person laughing at any point during any of his productions. It's almost difficult to call him overrated because everyone I know seems to agree with me on how terrible anything Tyler Perry creates is, but his movies and TV shows continue being made. And, oh yeah, Wikipedia (which is as far as I'm willing to go for research on this topic) claims that *Forbes* says that he was the highest-paid man in entertainment in 2011, earning $130 million. So clearly someone is watching these shows, and apparently enjoying them.

What the hell, people? Do you appreciate lowest-common-denominator humor that isn't even funny to the lowest denominator? Do you like your sitcoms written by someone who reads at a third-grade level? I once had a black friend suggest that the reason I don't appreciate Mr. Perry's work is because it's a racial thing; I'm white, and thus cannot understand his apparent genius. I just don't understand black humor, she told me. While I must admit I'm not even sure what "black humor" is, I am fairly certain I understand at least the fundamental levels of "humor," which is nonexistent in Perry works. I think it's less of a cultural thing and more of a thing about things that are funny, and Tyler Perry is not funny.

Blink 182

There are some pieces of pop culture that reach us at a certain point in our lives, and just seem to be *right* for us at that particular time and place. These things might not be *good* per se – often they have very little artistic value – but because they hit us at the right time, be it a stage of development or a specific age or even a physical location, we were able to appreciate them nonetheless. And as the years pass, even when we realize these things have considerably less value than we assigned them at the time, we are able to appreciate them due to the nostalgia they invoke and, often, good-natured humor. Limp Bizkit and *Field of Dreams* are two examples of this for me, and I bet most everyone has their own set.

Blink 182 is not one of these things. They are not good and never were. They kind of always sucked, actually, and when I look back on their work now, I feel no nostalgia, and neither should you. Blink basically capitalized on the 90s policy of doing as little as possible while playing music, and while it certainly worked at the time, let's not celebrate it now. Bands like Nirvana subscribed to this "Do Less" theory as well, but they were way less whiny than Blink 182, and thus are okay with me. In whatever sort of pop/punk/emo movement this was, Blink was the biggest of the big and the whiniest of the whiney, and I don't condone any of that. (And please, before you genre nerds jump on me and assert that "they weren't punk or emo or pop, they were actually mid-postpunk/modern expressionist," please save it. The labels mean nothing. I don't care). They were hailed as quirky and edgy back then, but in retrospect, "take off your pants and jacket" isn't really funny, and their drummer couldn't even succeed at being a reality TV personality, which is saying something.

Michelle Wie

Why do we still care? She has (at the time of this writing) two career LPGA tour victories. She's never won a major, and she has ONE top-ten finish in a major tournament in the last five years. The whole uncommonly young wunderkind/phenom thing has officially passed her by, and she's not even that good looking – zero Kournikova factor. And she plays women's golf. So why exactly are we supposed to be paying attention? Are we supposed to remember the 14-year-old who was going to change the sport of golf? All I remember was a spoiled brat who was preoccupied with playing PGA events (through sponsor exemptions) before she had ever won an LPGA event. She never even made the cut in one of those PGA tournaments, by the way, but she continued playing them. More cameras there, I guess. She also famously once said "I watch the PGA, not the LPGA. I like the players on the PGA better." What a bitch. In case you missed it the first time, this woman has two career LPGA wins. No majors.

Eric Clapton's Solo Career

This is tough for me, because I adore so much about Cream, Blind Faith, and Derek and the Dominos. But I have a social responsibility to call them like I see them, and as I see it, Clapton hasn't written or recorded much of value since the seventies.

Let me be perfectly clear: Eric Clapton is, at the very least, one of the 10 greatest rock and roll guitarists of all time. The Yardbirds were groundbreaking. *Layla and Other Assorted Love Songs* is a phenomenal album. And Cream is still one of the finest power trios in history. Clapton even gives the handful of us blues fans that still exist after the year 2000 a reason to live by organizing events like the Crossroads Guitar Festival. In fact, he was the first person inducted into the Rock & Roll Hall of Fame three separate times – with the Yardbirds, Cream, and then as a solo act. And it's that last one that's really the issue.

See, it's not that Clapton's solo stuff is bad; it's just not very good. Somewhere along the line, whether it was due to evolution as a musician or quitting hard drugs or just simple aging, the magic kind of left ol' Slowhand, at least regarding any studio recordings he's made. Oh he can still get up on stage and rock that Stratocaster, and the importance of this cannot be understated, at least in today's musical climate. It's why we keep him around. But the driving rock and lightning licks of the 60s are a thing of the past, and in their place are mostly slow ballads and easy listens. Nothing wrong with those things, they just aren't nearly as good as the early work. Somewhat ironically, he's spent the vast majority of his career as a solo artist – Cream only lasted about two years and the Yardbirds less than that, yet he's been schlepping it on his own for four damn decades. Sure, he's living off reputation at least a little bit at this point, but it's almost as if the Rock & Roll Hall of Fame people just finally relented. "Fine – he's a good musician, and though we don't really like any of the solo stuff that much, he's been doing it for so long. It MUST be worth something."

Plus he covered a Bob Marley song. Eric, I thought you were better than that.

It almost makes me wonder what would've happened if Jimi Hendrix wouldn't have died when he did. We tend to lionize guys like Hendrix, whose career was cut short and yet managed to pack so much outstanding and influential material in a tight window of time. Death at a young age adds a heavy amount of unknown to someone's legacy. There's a tendency to assume that untimely death means the individual in question had many more contributions to make, and only didn't because he or she ran out of time. But we never really think about the other option – what if Hendrix's musical career (or Duane Allman's or Stevie Ray Vaughan's or Janis Joplin's) just kind of slowly waned and fizzled out, like so many do? We give Jimi so much credit for advancing the way the electric guitar was played, and he deserves every damn bit of it. But what if he'd *lived*? We'll never know, but I do suspect if Clapton died of a heroin overdose in 1975, and Hendrix was still alive today, we might be thinking of both a lot differently.

Chris Brown

Ahhh I promised I wouldn't do it! But dammit, I just can't help myself. This is one R&B singer that needs to be singled out. And shot. If it wasn't enough that he assaulted my love Rihanna (and believe me, it was), he's been assaulting music listeners for years now. Even though I despise this musical genre in general, there's something that especially irks me about this tattooed jerk. Okay, it's probably the Rihanna thing. But wait! Then there's his obnoxious singing voice, his lack of any real creativity, his unbridled arrogance, and his tendency to engage in petulant Twitter fights. Chris Brown is really just one of those spoiled, overgrown children who tend to drift through celebrity and then disappear in a year or two. But he's still here! Why? Aren't there enough nasally pop singers with limited talent that essentially duplicate what he does, just without beating up my favorite human peacock?

I don't get it. Not only do we keep Chris Brown around, we give him Grammys – he took home one of the spares that were left in 2012 after Adele claimed her 92% share of the awards. This is not okay – we shouldn't be awarding being Chris Brown. Can't we just bring back Kris Kross and give them the Grammy instead? At least they had positive attitudes.

ALL UNDERRATED LIST, PART 1

I've told you who is overrated; now it's time to discuss those who get no respect. The unsung greats, the geniuses toiling in obscurity, the hard working, blue collar, middle class of celebrity and pop culture. Yes, it's time to talk about the underrated.

Now remember, this doesn't mean these things are unknown; just that they aren't given the credit they deserve. And again, they're in no particular order. To the list!

Cauliflower
Cauliflower has long since been the bastard cousin of broccoli, and this is not okay. Broccoli gets all the spotlight because it's *green*, and we're obsessed with green food in this godforsaken hippie health-freak organic culture we've built ourselves, but cauliflower is healthy as shit too. It, as my sources tell me, is "low in fat, low in carbs but high in dietary fiber, folate (which I think is a real thing), water, and vitamin C, possessing a high nutritional density." Yep, nutritional density. Read it and weep, broccoli crusaders.

It's a damn ball of nutrition.

Plus, it's a very versatile food. It has very little actual taste, just enough to keep it from being tasteless, and not too much to make it taste bad, which, being a vegetable, it almost certainly would, if it had more taste. Instead, this "minimalist taste" is delightfully usable, and lets you combine cauliflower with almost anything and get away with it. Seriously, name any dish and I can assure you that the addition of cauliflower will – at the very least – definitely probably not *ruin* it. And you can keep it simple too – even just combining it with melted cheese is a common favorite. It's delicious and makes your fat ass not feel quite so bad about housing what is essentially a bowl full of cheese. Hey, no need to feel bad at all – it's got nutritional density.

Silvertide

This is a band you probably haven't heard of, and that's not because I'm trying to pull some pretentious hipster shit on you. They were just never very well known, and didn't last very long. Silvertide saw a small glimpse of fame in 2004-05 when their one barely-popular single, "Aint Comin' Home," was played very occasionally on mainstream rock radio. They might've *released* subsequent singles, but nobody really paid attention. And then they broke up – their career spanned one album.

Why am I telling you this? Because Silvertide f'ing rocked. That one album, *Show and Tell*, was 11 tracks of blistering, stupid, straightforward rock and roll, and that is something that was painfully absent through most of that particular decade. For me, it was an oasis in a desert of indie rock and easy listenings, and a godsend. They were my new favorite band.

Of course, it ended there, and was seemingly over before it started. There was no second album, as all the band members parted ways to form or participate in other projects, which uniformly sucked (trust me, I've checked). But I still listen to *Show and Tell*; it's a naïve, underdeveloped, and massively flawed album, but maybe that's okay. My musical tastes have changed, and I no longer cling to loud, frantic guitar licks and shrill vocals like I used to, but I can still see the good in an album like this. It falls somewhere between 80s hair metal and modern day mainstream, wannabe rock, and that's not a terrible place to be.

Bill Bryson

Based on how many books he's sold I'd assume everyone on earth has heard of him, but that is apparently not the case. I stumbled upon his wilderness masterpiece *A Walk in the Woods* a few years ago and immediately adopted Bryson as my new favorite author. And not being one to shut the hell up about things, I of course told everyone about it and was surprised to find a lot of people who hadn't heard of him either. Well, regarding Bryson's writings: if you have the means, I highly recommend picking one up. (And yes, you do have the means; your local library will have them, and I've recently found that libraries give out books for free. Not sure how they're able to sustain this business model, but I plan on taking advantage until they wise up.)

Bill Bryson is smart, quick witted, hilarious, keenly observational, well-researched, and blatantly honest. Born in America (the great state of Iowa, to be exact), he moved to Europe and resided there for 30 years before finally coming back home. So right there, there's something for everyone: the unashamed American nationalists who probably own guns, and the conceited, tea-drinking neck-beard people who are convinced Europe is *"sooooo much more cultured"* and better than America despite the fact that they continue to –and always will – live here. Both of these groups will enjoy Bryson – he breaks down walls.

The book in question, *A Walk in the Woods*, takes place just after his return stateside, when he attempts to "rediscover America" on the Appalachian Trail. Between his astute observations, lovable curmudgeon streak, and the fact that he is blatantly unequipped to hike anything, much less something as daunting as the AT, it makes for a great read.

Otters

Much like cauliflower, they've been the maligned stepchild of another creature for most of history. In the animal kingdom, the beaver seems to get all the credit, while the otter is routinely an afterthought. This is horseshit. Yes, beavers are much more hardworking and understanding of middle-class American values – it seems they never take a break from working on those dams, night and day. But that's their flaw as well: beavers do not understand the work/life balance, and the singular goal of dam building consumes their lives and gives them one-track minds. These beavers are not well-rounded individuals.

Otters, on the other hand, live life at a different pace. They aren't concerned with dam building, oil wells, gold mines, or real estate; they mostly go wherever the tides take them. Indeed, otters can usually be seen floating leisurely on their backs, cracking crabs on their chests and basking in life's beautiful glow. Their priorities are different. Clearly otters, along with koalas, are the hippies of the animal kingdom. But unlike human hippies, who commonly have dreadlocks and poor hygiene, the animal hippies stay groomed and work when they have to. They just understand there's more to life than building homes or constantly hunting. We could all learn something from the otter.

A MAN NAMED PLAXICO

(Originally written just after Plaxico Burress was released from prison.)

On Monday of this week, Plaxico Burress was released from prison after serving two years. For those of you who don't know, Burress is an NFL receiver who spent nine mostly successful seasons with the Pittsburgh Steelers and New York Giants. As of June 7, 2011, he had 505 career receptions, 7,845 receiving yards, and 55 touchdowns. Burress also caught the game-winning touchdown in Super Bowl XLII to defeat the previously unbeaten New England Patriots. And he spent two years in federal prison for shooting himself in the leg.

Well, sort of. A brief history of the event: one night in 2008, ol' Plax thought it a good idea to visit a New York City nightclub with his Glock pistol tucked in the waistband of his sweatpants. Clearly the greatest transgression here is a grown man wearing sweatpants out to a club, but the gun idea wasn't brilliant either, because, well, it's a gun, which is made to shoot things, and generally shooting things in a major urban area carries at least some sort of

QUITTING COLD STONE (AND OTHER STRUGGLES)

penalty. Also, he did have a concealed carry license, though it was for the state of Florida, not New York. And it was expired. Close, but no cigar.

As the story goes, the gun started to slide down Plaxico's leg at one point during the night. He reached down to stop it, and in doing so accidentally pulled the trigger, for the gun fired and put a bullet in his right thigh. Presumably this caused some sort of uproar in the club, possibly a few drinks were spilled and the less-attractive women were forced to put their tops back on. Plaxico headed straight to the hospital, was treated for the wound and released the following afternoon. The injury turned out to be not all that serious, and it appeared he would be able to return to football activities in the near future. You might say he dodged a bullet in the figurative sense, even though literally he did just the opposite.

However, there was a problem: carrying a gun without a permit is apparently illegal. Plaxico knew this – or at least his advisors did – and he turned himself in to police after being released from the hospital. Law enforcement made it very clear they would charge him with criminal possession of a weapon – a felony. Even New York mayor Michael Bloomberg got in on the action, insisting that Burress be prosecuted to the full extent of the law, saying that anything less than the max penalty of three and a half years in prison would be a "mockery of the law." *Well shit*, you could almost hear Plaxico saying to himself, *I'd like to have a do-over on THAT one. Also, my leg kinda hurts.*

Burress was suspended by his team for the rest of the season without pay, and eventually was indicted on two counts of criminal possession of a weapon in the second degree and a single count of reckless endangerment in the second degree, both felonies. He agreed to a plea deal that would put him in the big house for two years. And that brings us to today.

Now, I understand the severity of the charges, but I'm not sure I understand the severity of the crime. Two years for shooting...himself? No, he did not have a valid license to carry the gun, but is that really worth 24 months in the slammer? I can't imagine what a man without Burress' financial resources would've ended up with in the same scenario. And really, hadn't he already punished himself enough? As my man Chuck Klosterman said about the ordeal:

I don't know what the punishment for carrying a concealed weapon without a permit should be, but it shouldn't be any worse than, say, getting shot in the leg, and that already fucking happened.

Clearly Burress isn't the brightest individual. I'm sure many of you would like to like to file criminal charges for the simple fact that his name is Plaxico, and while I'm inclined to agree with you, I think we should place the blame on the parents in that case. Still, the man is no choir boy; he's been involved in domestic disturbance calls and fined and suspended numerous times by his NFL teams for various reasons. Not exactly an upstanding citizen, but I don't see the connection between any of that and the leg-shooting incident. Two years for carrying a weapon that was purchased legally. And he had no previous gun charges.

The situation only becomes more head scratching when juxtaposed with the curious case of Donte Stallworth. Also an NFL receiver, Stallworth received a mere 30 days in jail for DUI manslaughter. Yes, he killed a pedestrian while driving drunk and served less than a month. Many reasons were given for why the sentence was so light:

Miami-Dade State Attorney Katherine Fernandez Rundle cited Stallworth's lack of previous criminal record, cooperation with police and willingness to accept responsibility as factors in the plea deal.

The story also notes an "undisclosed financial settlement" with the victim's family in order to avoid a lawsuit. Sounds about right. So the family got paid and didn't sue,

QUITTING COLD STONE (AND OTHER STRUGGLES)

and while I fail to see how any sum of money will heal the wounds of a dead loved one, that's just how the legal system shakes out sometimes. But then Burress wasn't sued by anyone either; prosecuted by the government, just as Stallworth was, and yet the huge discrepancy in the sentences.

Let's look at the factors, and how they applied to Burress:

Cooperation with prosecutors: He turned himself in to police a day after the incident.

Lack of criminal record: Two domestic disturbance calls, never any charges filed.

Willingness to accept responsibility: Did you see the bullet hole in his leg? Kinda hard not to accept that.

Making good with the victim/family: Well, the victim here was his right leg. Sure seems like he did everything to rectify the situation – got prompt medical treatment, probably took antibiotics, continued using the leg as soon as possible. I'm not sure if there was a financial settlement involved, but it seems unlikely that a person's leg would have much use for money anyway.

I'm not attempting to defend a pampered professional athlete here, nor do I want to further incriminate one. It just seems like an odd comparison. If we let one DUI manslaughter off the hook, why send someone away for two years when his only crime was friendly fire? Is that really the best use of our national resources and tax dollars? Why not just shoot him in the other leg and call it good? Who's making these rules?

(Update: Burress did indeed make a return to the NFL following prison time, and signed a one-year contract with the New York Jets in 2011. He had, by most any measure, an above-average season with 45 catches and eight touchdowns. Burress was not resigned by the Jets and did not play the majority of the 2012 season, but late in the year was

picked up by the Steelers to supplement their injury-depleted receiving corps. He played 4 games with the team, catching 3 passes for 42 yards and a touchdown. He was using both legs.)

THE FIRST DAY OF SCHOOL

I can think of no event in my adult life that is – or will ever be – so simultaneously exciting and terrifying as the first day of school was in my adolescence. From grade school to high school, the emotions that accompanied Day One of each new year seemed to be more prominent than those of the rest of the days combined.

These emotions can be broken down into three categories:

Sadness. It is, after all, the end of an era, a wonderful time of freedom and expression that can never be replicated elsewhere in life: summer vacation. Those three months of bliss – especially in the early years, when summer jobs are still far off on the horizon, and the days consist of nothing but waking up at 10 and running barefoot through the neighborhood – are the childhood equivalent of winning the lottery once a year. It was amazing; limited responsibility and limitless Kool-Aid, a kid could be a kid during the summer.

I don't recall looking at a clock much at all in these times, for there was no reason to do so. I'd roll out of bed whenever I damn well pleased, accompanied by the sun shining into my bedroom window and the chirping of birds outside. There were no alarms. I would walk downstairs in my sleeping attire with hair pushed up to one side and slosh together a bowl of cereal. There might be a note from my mother, kindly asking my brothers and me to help out with a few quick chores during the day. We would consider it. Often I'd plop down in front of the computer and numb my brain with Command & Conquer or some similar game for an hour or two, before stumbling outside and running around in the woods or jumping in the lake with some neighborhood folk. When the evening came, the parents would return to our castle and we'd all convene for dinner. It was burgers on the stovetop or sometimes ribs on the grill, with a side of the gigantic and delicious corn on the cob they'd bought from an old farmer on the side of the road, all slathered in butter and sprinkled with salt. (The corn, not the farmer). Bedtime was whenever I decided, and the glorious cycle would repeat again.

Then one day, summer began to wane. The days got a little shorter, grown-ups began to whisper of autumn, and on TV, retail shops started to run commercials highlighting the disgusting notion of "Back to School." I guess we all knew it was coming, but as the calendar slowly counted down to Day One, a feeling of helplessness encroached. The last few weeks of summer were almost unenjoyable, for we knew what lied ahead. School gripped my mind and wouldn't even let me take solace in my precious remaining days. It was over.

Anticipation. Meanwhile, this summer countdown created a tremendous buildup to the first day of school. In the earlier days, it wasn't as big a deal; I just knew I'd be subjected to nine months of boredom and unholy wakeup calls. But around the time I hit junior high, everything changed.

QUITTING COLD STONE (AND OTHER STRUGGLES)

Suddenly there were expectations. Social expectations. The actual class part wasn't much different, but interacting with my peers for some reason became a whole different ballgame. I couldn't just show up wearing whatever I wanted and talk to whomever I wanted about whatever I wanted. No, there was a social hierarchy now, and I'd better do my best to start climbing. Otherwise, a life of certain misery awaited. At least that's what they told me.

Who told me? I don't actually know. But somehow, we all just kind of accepted it as the way things were. Life was now about the pursuit of "cool." For some – the in-crowd – this came naturally. For me, it did not.

So I tried. This meant changing the way I dressed – and actually giving a shit. Back-to-school clothes shopping became more important than Super Bowl Sunday; I had one chance to buy my wardrobe for the coming year, and I'd better not screw it up. I would spend hours at the mall with my mother, trying on t-shirts and baggy jeans from Pacific Sunwear and Zumiez and other stores that specialized in the "skater" look. That was my thing in those days, which now seems odd, considering I didn't really like skateboarding.

The reason for this, as I recall, was a single bus ride before my sixth-grade year. It was nearing the end of summer, with the start of school looming, and I was being shuttled somewhere (the exact location unimportant) for some church youth group function, if memory serves. I was sitting next to my best friend, same age as me and presumably as frightened about the newfound expectations to be cool as I. Out of nowhere, an eighth-grader – a seasoned vet in the social challenges of middle school – turned around and posed us a question.

"So," he asked, "what are you guys?"

"What?" I responded. What *were* we? Like, in what context? Species-wise? Homo sapien, thank you sir.

"Like, what *are* you guys? Are you jocks, are you preps, or are you skaters?"

That was literally all he said, and it certainly suggested those were the only three options. Since he'd been around the block and was assumedly an expert in these things, I believed him. I'd never given it much thought before that point, so I wasn't able to provide him an answer. But I knew damn well that I'd better have one by the first day of school.

So I pondered it. What was I, really? Honestly, I was none of those things – I was a skinny kid who liked Coca-Cola and video games – but it seemed I'd have to select one from the list. At least they weren't making me pick Democrat or Republican yet. Well, I didn't play sports, so jock was out. I definitely didn't want to be preppy, because I considered them total dorks who wore sweater vests. So that left skater. I thought about it and decided I could get used to the idea. It seemed harmless. So despite the fact that I didn't own a skateboard, had never really ridden one, and wasn't making any plans to do so in the future, I billed myself as a skater, and dressed (and shopped) as such.

The clothes, of course, did not come out until Day One of school; it would be like performing scenes from a play before opening night. It wouldn't be right – they were to be saved until their grand debut. When the store employee asked if I wanted to wear my new shoes (Etnies or Osiris or some other skate brand) out of the store, I dismissed him with a scoff and a wave of the hand. I wasn't going to waste the first wear someplace no one would see it. Same went for the shirts and pants – they hung untouched in my closet until Day One.

I meticulously planned what I would wear the first week. Day One – opening night – was of course reserved for the coolest outfit of the lot. One needed to make an impression, so I made sure the best combination was ready for the first day of school. Day Two brought out my top backups, clothes not quite as fly as the first ensemble but still new, fresh, and confidence-inspiring. After that I'd gradually phase in any other new items I had until I was wearing last year's gear by the end of the week. Then, I'd mix and match shirts and pants and do it all again the next week. It was a solid system to cover up the fact that I didn't actually have many clothes.

Fear. And all of it culminated in one gigantic, shivering ball of fear. The onset of another school year was above all else terrifying, as I lied in my bed the night before and stressed uncontrollably about early wakeup times, menial assignments, and whether my hair, build, and facial complexion would be up to snuff. Whether my coolness was discreetly downgraded at some point over the summer without anyone telling me. Whether any young ladies would take a shine to me this year, or whether I'd just be standing in the corner again, hands in pockets, at the middle school dances. Whether my small group of friends would still be my friends, or whether they'd turn on me.

Any fear about validation from your peers is a tough one to deal with, because no matter what you do, you have no real control over it. This was my – and I suspect many people's – fear in school.

And when the first day of school actually came, most of my fears weren't actually realized. Oh, things were different – classrooms, teachers, girls' hair colors – but for the most part, nothing changed too drastically. I still hated being in school (anyone who tells you they don't is lying or Communist), but as the weeks went by and I settled in, each year became roughly as tolerable as the last. But when school let out, and summer vacation ran its inevitable course, the feelings would begin to creep in again.

Sadness. Anticipation. Fear. It's the cycle of the coming school year.

THE WONDERS OF BOB ROSS

Turn off your phone.

Slip into some comfy clothes, take the lights down low, and grab a glass of wine, scotch, or something equally ~~alcoholic~~ satisfying. Get away from the noises of life, isolate yourself for a minute, and come away with me. Allow yourself to be swept up into the magical world of one of the great masters:

Bob Ross.

A painter, a visionary, an afro. The "Happy Trees" man, as you may know him, has been underappreciated since the time his television program first went on air in 1983. Yes, he has reached cult status for his hairstyle and calmingly idiosyncratic way of describing nature, and has made his way on to t-shirts, painting supplies, and YouTube auto-tune remixes. These things are good, but Robert Norman Ross deserves to be appreciated in a different light, for he is a beautiful soul and a brilliant artist.

"The Joy of Painting," Bob's TV show, was aired on PBS for more than a decade straight. For 403 total episodes, he walked us through his simple process for creating beautiful nature paintings, and somehow made us believe that we could do it too. Using his now-famous "wet-on-wet" technique, Ross would make fantastic little paintings in under a half an hour, featuring happy little mountains, ponds, and clouds.

He was as encouraging as he was calming. Always using a limited palette – so that it would be easy for us to paint along with him – Ross assured us that it was our world, and that there were "no rules here." He never wanted us to copy or trace, but to take what was inside of us and put it on canvas. "Anyone can paint," Bob would say, dispelling the perceived need for formal training or God-given talent. "I believe that we all have a picture inside of us." And always more important than what he said was how he said it.

And oh, how he said it. Bob's true gift was the mesmerizing way he spoke as he walked us through the process. Barely above a whisper, his gentle voice guided us across the canvas, always reassuring us that we can do it. "This is your world," he'd say. "You can do anything you want to. So maybe, over here, there lives a happy little bush." Calmly and quietly, he would mix Pthalo Green with the least little touch of Van Dyke Brown on his palette, and tap the canvas creating a perfect row of bushes or trees or rocks, almost effortlessly. "Just tap it," he'd say in a hushed tone. "There. There."

While his simple painting style is remarkable in its own right – usually starting with a few seemingly unconnected blotches of color, and turning into a beautiful mountain scene, always in about 26 minutes – the vast majority of viewers (some 80 million per week in the show's prime) had no interest in learning how to paint. No, we watched simply because we were drawn to Bob and his enchantingly positive ways. Inviting Bob Ross into your home meant 30 minutes without politics, war, or hate. He had little use for these things, and you never really got the idea he even gave them much thought. Bob just wanted to paint. "I believe," he'd tell us, "every day is a good day when you paint." And so he did.

Robert Norman Ross was born in Orlando, Florida, in 1942. After graduating high school, he enlisted in the United States Air Force and was shipped to Alaska. This was the first time he'd ever seen mountains, snow, and pine trees, which all became staples of his work. He had little free time, so he developed his quick painting style out of necessity.

"I used to go home at lunch and do a couple while I had my sandwich," Ross told the Orlando Sentinel in an interview before his death. "I'd take them back that afternoon and sell them."

Soon, he was seeing more money from painting than he was from his Air Force paycheck. Ross started to see it as a viable career option when he left the military. Because he'd had about enough of the Air Force, anyway; he didn't like being mean.

"I was the guy who makes you scrub the latrine, the guy who makes you make your bed, the guy who screams at you for being late to work," Ross said in the same interview. "The job requires you to be a mean, tough person. And I was fed up with it. I promised myself that if I ever got away from it, it wasn't going to be that way anymore."

For anyone who's ever seen "The Joy of Painting," picturing Bob Ross screaming is almost impossible. But unlike the unsubstantiated urban myth of PBS's Mister Rogers duty as a Marine sniper, Ross' military career was very real and spanned 20 years. So when he finally retired in 1981, he vowed to never raise his voice in anger again. He began teaching art for a national art supply company, and within a year began his own art business. It lost $20,000 in the first 12 months.

Undaunted, Bob took his talents to television. Initially nobody would give him a look (could've been the hair), but eventually a public TV station in Falls Church, Virginia, gave him a pilot. Once the show started airing, PBS stations around the country rushed to pick up "The Joy" as

QUITTING COLD STONE (AND OTHER STRUGGLES)

well. They had seen the light, and the American public would soon follow.

A year later Bob found his permanent home at a tiny PBS affiliate in Muncie, Indiana. The station promised him complete creative freedom and made good on its word, as Ross recorded every show there for the next 12 years. It was an extremely simple operation – always the same three-camera shoot on a black background, Bob always wearing jeans, an open-collared button-down, and that delightfully bushy afro – but the genius was in the simplicity. Just a blank canvas, a dozen or so paints, and Bob's hypnotic voice to take us through the creation of another beautiful painting. Repeated some 400 times, it left a legacy of happy little clouds, mountains, trees, and comatose human beings. It is to this day the most calming show in television history.

Bob got the formula down so well that eventually he and his crew could pound out a whole series – 13 shows – in just over two days. He always insisted there were no edits.

"The Joy of Painting" was technically an instruction show, but the reason it wasn't usually viewed as such is because it lacked a whole lot of...well, instruction. Sure, we got to see the painting happen from start to finish, but watching a seasoned painter paint is like watching the hands of an accomplished guitarist; even if I can see what he's doing, it doesn't mean I'm going to be able to do it anytime soon. He'd occasionally give out some vague instructions like "follow your angles" when painting mountains, whatever the hell that meant. But most of the time, it was just us watching him paint, and him assuring us we could do it.

And really, that's all we wanted. I didn't want to learn how to paint and neither did most other viewers, and that's why we didn't give a damn that he never told us *why* he combined Alizarin Crimson and Titanium White to make a big ol' boulder. We just watched him mix whatever paints he chose, and it always turned out perfect. If, of course, we were awake at the end of the show.

Bob Ross died of lymphoma in 1995. He was 52, but his soul was much older. His art has been criticized for its simplicity, and for being "childish" or "reductionist," and Bob was always the first to admit that none of his paintings would hang in the Smithsonian. But he didn't care; he loved painting, and firmly believed it would "bring a lot of good thoughts to your heart." And he just wanted to share that with us, and convince us we could get in on the action. The man was completely without pretense, and in a world of turned-up noses and white wine, I think that's something we needed, and still need. Bob showed us that art is not just for "artists," and we can do anything we want. "Believe that you can do it," he would say, "because you can do it."

Bob wanted us to believe in ourselves, and to think happy thoughts. These are the same elementary concepts we learned when we were children, but were somewhere along the way convinced to toss by the wayside due to their "impractical" or "unrealistic" nature. But why? Why can't we fill ourselves with child-like belief? What harm does it cause? We've had the irrational exuberance beaten out of us over time, and as adults we're supposed to only entertain "normal" ideas. But normal is boring, and it is – by definition – not special. Bob was special, and he knew you could be too. I, for one, choose to believe him.

Any motivational speaker will tell you that most success comes not from physical or intellectual superiority, but from winning the battle in your own head; self-confidence, mental toughness, and resilience. Bob taught us the same thing, but he just made it more fun. "There are no limits here," he'd often say. And he believed it. Why can't we?

THE TIPPING POINT

I've come around on tipping. Not long ago I was a total curmudgeon when it came to gratuity, and most of my policies on the subject were reminiscent of a shriveled and bitter 80 year-old man. "Why the hell should I tip her for doing an average job?" I would growl. "Doesn't that contradict the very idea of a tip?" Indeed, I did have a point; it is fairly ridiculous that we as a society consider anything under 15% (at least in restaurant situations) a "bad" tip. In other words, if I make a donation of *only* an extra 12% of the total bill to the waitress' personal booze/tattoo fund, it is assumed that I am either **a)** unhappy with the service rendered and making a statement about it with my money, **b)** a cheapskate, disrespectful slob, or all-around asshole, or **c)** all of the above.

Keep in mind in this scenario I'm kicking in a little extra for no reason other than the fact that she executed the job she's already being paid to do with remarkable mediocrity. For some reason, however, these are the rules we've all agreed to follow.

Mini-rants aside, my stance has softened. For whatever reason – probably apathy – I've tapped the brakes on fighting the good fight and decided, more or less, to conform. There are too many legit issues requiring our attention – like people leaving their carts in the middle of the grocery store parking lot – to get bent out of shape about adding a few extra bucks to the tab even if the waitress or waiter didn't actually earn it. I get it; it's a societal norm, servers make most of their money off tips, and it does still provide some sliver of incentive to do an above-average job. No reason to raise a ruckus here. I'll play the game and we can all be happy.

But alas, the story doesn't end there. There have been new developments on the tipping front, and they require our attention. Gratuity solicitation has found its way to a new place altogether: the register.

All of a sudden it seems as if every sandwich shop, coffee house, and Cold Stone Creamery (gah!) has latched on to a new passive-aggressive tipping campaign. The situation usually unfolds as follows:

I enter one of the aforementioned establishments to buy a sandwich, coffee, or birthday cake remix ice cream treat.

I step to the counter and make my order, which the cheery employee quickly fulfills.

I am handed my item and asked for a form of payment. I hand over my debit card, for unlike Randy Moss, I rarely carry cash.

The employee runs the card and hands me a receipt. "Just need your signature at the bottom," they say with a smile.

I look at the receipt. There are 3 lines: one for my signature as promised, one for my voluntary tip, and one for the full total, including voluntary tip. These are the same receipts commonly seen in bars and sit down restaurants, i.e. places you would actually leave a tip.

I wage a split-second internal battle over whether or not to write down anything next to "gratuity." After all, I would never usually leave a tip in this situation – nothing was delivered nor was I waited on. I simply made a quick transaction with a cash register and a pimple-faced high school kid wearing an apron. Why would I tip for that? It's the lowest form of retail. Do I tip the person who rings up my clearance Arizona jeans at J.C. Penney? No. But still, the fact that there is a full line devoted to a tip almost makes it seems like I *should* enter something. What does everyone else do in this situation? I briefly consider polling the other customers.

I decide against this gonzo tip and hand the receipt back with only my signature. After all, that's all they asked for.

The employee takes the receipt and thanks me. "Have a good day," I say as I grab my item and turn to leave. It is at this point when the employee looks at the receipt, sees that there is no tip, and looks back up at me. The sunny disposition instantly fades and is replaced by a partial frown and vague look of contempt. "Yeah," they mumble with no emotion, "you too." This last part is barely audible.

This same situation plays out time and time again, yet my actions stay the same. I'm sorry, I just can't justify leaving a tip for such a simple transaction. In many cases, the reason I drove to the store instead of opting for delivery was to *avoid* a tip in the first place. Man has made these particular purchases tip-free for millennia, and there has never been an issue, yet all of a sudden this needs to change? And what's with the attitude from the cashier at the end there? Why do they look at me like I just punted their poodle across the street? Were they actually *expecting* a tip?

Many questions, few answers. I assume it will remain this way until I – along with everyone else – just conform to the demands of medium-sized business and scrawl "$2.00" on that tip line. Until then, I will no doubt continue to be a massive disappointment to minimum wage high schoolers everywhere.

I'M FEELING SKINNY, TONY

Heavyweights is the greatest film of all time. This is purely a statement of personal preference, but it is not an opinion; something that feels this undeniable can't be anything other than fact. When asked to list my favorite movies, I feel compelled to mention that *Heavyweights* is number one and everything else is residual. Simply put, the movie is a masterpiece, a piece of art so divine that it can only be the work of God himself. Walt Disney Pictures claims ownership, but this is a farce, for no one entity can truly own this film any more than one can own the sun, sky, or oceans. *Heavyweights* belongs to all of us.

The plot is simple: a bunch of overweight youngsters are shipped to a summer camp with the goal of getting their weight under control. The veteran campers are not worried in the beginning; they have developed a system of staying well fed, minimally active, and generally obese throughout the summer, leading to their return year after year. The camp owners – the Bushkins – do little to hold the kids' feet to the fire; they seem content to buy them go-karts, jet skis, and large inflatable water toys while watching them enjoy the hell out of the summer and neglect any form of weight loss. This all changes when the camp is bought by Tony Perkis (Ben Stiller, before he was Ben Stiller), an overbearing fitness freak determined to whip the little fatasses into shape. All hell breaks loose, the campers mutiny, and general hilarity ensues. Also there's a hot nurse.

If you are an inferior cinema mind and haven't seen *Heavyweights*, you might ask why I hold this movie in such high regard. Well, it has everything:

Fat people

More specifically, fat *children*. As I've already made abundantly clear, fat people are funnier than the general population; they need to be funny to make up for their physical situation. It's natural selection, really. But fat children are funnier yet, with their underdeveloped social skills, irrationally optimistic views on life, and chubby cheeks. Naturally, *Heavyweights* is full of fat children – it is after all a movie about a fat camp – and it utilizes them to the max. Aside from the obvious curb appeal of lead man Gerald Garner (age 11, 141 lbs) and his phenomenal side-part, the movie also features a young Keenan Thompson as Roy, and Shaun Weiss – best known for his work as Goldberg in *Mighty Ducks* – as Josh. A star-studded cast, all plump, young, lovable, and hilarious.

And let's not forget camp counselor Pat Finley, who is repeatedly berated by Tony Perkis throughout the film until the end when he overcomes and hooks up with Julie the hot nurse. I'm giving their relationship credit for setting off the rash of "fat guy with hot wife" sitcoms the past 10 years (*King of Queens, According to Jim, Grounded for Life*, even *Family Guy*).

A packing/unpacking montage

Always a good idea, executed to perfection here. When Gerry makes his first visit to the Chipmunk bunk – early on in the movie, while the going is still good at Camp

Hope – Josh introduces him to the Chipmunk way of doing things. "Chiiiiiiiiiiipmunks, download NOW!" the robust boy commands, setting off a flurry of activity in which the other portly adolescents rush around the room in double time, showing off and stowing the delicious sugary treats they've brought for the summer. They strategically stuff every nook and cranny of the bunk with candy bars, pastries, and deli meats. It's worth the price of admission alone.

Tony Perkis
Played by Ben Stiller, in undoubtedly his greatest yet least celebrated major role ever. Tony is the classic villain, ruling Camp Hope with an iron fist and not allowing even a shred of positivity to creep into the campers' lives. He even has his version of the SS – Team Perkis – to do his bidding and eradicate all candy and fatty food from the grounds. We come to find out that Tony's intention is to make and sell an infomercial out of the kids' weight loss that summer, and when things don't go according to plan, he begins to lose it.

A certain member of Team Perkis *does* play a crucial role in ensuring all the campers are using the buddy system during swim time, possibly their one redeeming quality. Which brings me to...

An obliviously funny foreigner
Lars. Dear god, Lars. He is the perfect comic relief – clueless and hopelessly devoted to Tony, he acts as the tyrant's right-hand man. He also has a funny accent, which is a good bet to make 11 year-olds (and me) consistently laugh. We never even learn where he's actually from; only, as he puts it, "far away."

Lars takes over for Pat as counselor of the Chipmunk bunk, much to Pat's chagrin. The scene in which he introduces himself to the campers is possibly the best of the film, and thus, the best scene in the history of Hollywood.

Google it. Immediately.

A David beats Goliath moment

I assume this cliché still works if David is actually bigger than Goliath, which is the case here. At the end of the summer, the kids are forced into a competition of skill known as the Apache Relay against neighboring Camp MVP, the jock camp. As one would assume, they get their large, round asses neatly kicked each year, but this summer is different. Through sheer willpower, an eclectic skill set, and the cunning orchestration of Pat Finley, Camp Hope finally wins the Apache Relay, and we are all along for the ride. The race culminates in Gerry actualizing his lifelong dream of driving a go-kart as he beats a skilled driver from Camp MVP by jumping clear over him at the end of an epic race. And if you would like to raise the point that this might be a tad unrealistic given Gerry has never driven a go-kart in his life, you can go fuck off somewhere. Gerry had it in him, I'm sure of it.

Inexplicably the Apache Relay is not on YouTube. A damn shame. I would go through the process of putting this clip up myself, but nobody actually puts any videos on YouTube. We just wait for other people to do it.

Moral of the story? If you want to experience the finest in American cinema, watch *Heavyweights*. If you've already seen it, watch it again, for I assure you it gets better with each viewing. My brothers and I watched the VHS until the tape began to wear out, and then we watched it some more, filling in the quotes of any parts that might be damaged. We couldn't help but gravitate to its genius. My life will forever be changed by the day my father came home from the video store, put the VHS tape in the VCR, and hit play.

Well done, Mr. Neumann. Well done.

STATUS ABUSE

Mother of God, THEY'VE CHANGED IT AGAIN!
There I was, minding my own business and carelessly clicking on the Facebook shortcut for the 787th time today, and what do I see when the page loads? Carnage. It's completely different! The things that were over there are over here now, and the things that were over here...well shit, I can't find them anywhere! How the hell am I supposed to know whose birthday it is? This is complete and utter chaos – the stock markets will surely drop because of it. My god, another recession is coming! Why would you do this to us Mark Zuckerberg? Do you hate us? DO YOU HATE AMERICA???

This is a summation of some statuses I've seen since Facebook made a few minor changes to its layout this week. It happens once every twelve months or so – The 'Book does a subtle redesign to shake things up a little and ultimately improve functionality, and The People of Facebook collectively react as if a cow had jumped in their bathtub. In reality there isn't much difference from the previous version, but that doesn't seem to matter. Why would they change a perfectly good thing? the people moan. It's as if we expect the developers to consult with each of us individually before making any changes. The irony, of course, is that in another twelve months when Facebook does another minor redesign, we'll collectively freak out again and long for the days of THIS version. The one we're currently condemning. It's a vicious cycle.

Anyway, this public outcry made me think about other stupid things people do with their statuses. Be it worthless, obnoxious, or mind-numbingly repetitive, there is a lot of Facebook status garbage out there. I call it status abuse, and it annoys the hell out of me, just as I'm sure it does many of you. Disclaimer: yes, I know I am under no obligation to read or expose myself to other people's statuses or Facebook altogether, just as the layout change bitchers are not required to visit the website at all if they find it unsatisfactory. Nobody is holding a gun to our heads – we have complete autonomy to use Facebook as much or as little as we want. But let's be real: we're all hopelessly addicted, so there's no way we're gonna quit. It's like nicotine, and there's no Facebook patch. So instead? We come back again and again, and piss and moan about what we don't like. It's just easier that way, and I'm totally okay with the arrangement.

So, commence pissing. Commence moaning. Here's a (certainly not exhaustive) list of status abuses; things that if people stopped doing, it would make the digital world just a hair better:

Ugh I'm so bored! – While I'm sure you are, since you're spending your time writing something so inconsequential on a website, this has no meaning. You're bored. Great. Why do you think we need this information? What are we to do with it? I do not care how bored you are, just as I do not care how tired you are. These are things we all experience, but do not need to be shared with the digital world. Please save your posts for something at least marginally in the same neighborhood as interesting. Also, "ugh" is not a word. It just sounds like you're pooping.

Working till 4, going to the gym, then having dinner – This is not a status; this is a summary of your day. Again, pointless. Those who need to know what you're doing – anyone actually involved in your day-to-day life – will already know your personal itinerary. The rest of us don't give a fuck.

Looking forward to the weekend! – We all are.

(a constant barrage of pictures/posts about your infant or toddler) – Listen, I get it. You're a mother/father, and your child is your life. It's how it works, and that's great. But please try to realize your child isn't everyone's life. If they do something of actual note or something truly funny, by all means share it with us. But playing flag football or trying on Dad's hat do not count. In these cases, keep it in house. Tell your spouse and move on. And all those people commenting on how cute your kid is? They're just being nice. Sorry.

Why does everything always turn out like this? – Ah yes, the classic vague downer fishing for sympathy. If you're gonna publicly feel sorry for yourself, at least literally tell us what's going on. We still don't care, but that would be slightly interesting. But simply posting a few ambiguous words about how unhappy you are, and hoping someone asks for more info – that's just pathetic. How insecure can we be, people?

BELIEVE in yourself and you can reach your goals. A LITTLE belief goes a LONG way! Go for it! Reach for the stars! – The exact opposite of the previous category, but just as obnoxious. I appreciate what you're trying to do – spreading positivity is admirable – but this is not really the place for it. The inspirational quotes and pictures have become a Facebook cliché, so much that they seem to be taking over the majority of my news feed. At some point – a point we've long since passed – it just becomes noise, like Charlie Brown's parents, and the reader begins to tune it out. Maybe it would resonate more if the phrases and quotes were actually good, but more often than not they're just a few buzz words in all caps surrounded by exclamation points. BELIEVE that you can DO something original!!!!!

LOL – Stop. Just stop. This has gone on long enough. You are not laughing out loud. So stop. For god's sake just stop.
Stop.

(song lyrics) – I love music just as much as the next guy, so I completely understand how song lyrics can make you feel, and why you'd want to share that feeling. But when will we finally realize that words sung over a tune do not translate to text in a status box? Even if the reader knows the song and the lyrics, the feeling doesn't transfer. It usually just ends up looking like a poorly constructed sentence. Which reminds me...

thought i'd hed over to smittys and get a beer anyone want to join meeet me over their should be a god time after thatwe can hit the trails or whatever anywon wanna come jis hit me up on the cel – I get that this is the internet; I'm not asking for perfect grammar and punctuation. But for shit's sake have some self-respect. This looks like you vomited your status.

(self-pictures) – You know, a single person holding out the camera and pointing it back at themselves (or taking it in the mirror, same thing) for no real reason, other than to show the world how good they look. Often called "selfies." Usually alone in their home or a random location. This does not make you look fun or pretty, just lonely and insecure.

Down 25 pts in my fantasy league but got Brady playing tonight. Come on Pats! – Hey, I'm as guilty as anyone of oversharing about fantasy football. But what we need to accept, fantasy players of the world, is that nobody cares about our fantasy team but us. Really, it's less interesting than Chris Daughtry. Share with people in your league, nobody else.

Headed to the show with @JennyMarquis @PaulDzzz, gonna be crazy! #Aintnostoppingusnow – Wrong website. This isn't Twitter.

YOUR SPORT PREFERENCE OFFENDS ME

(Written in early 2011, just after (as the first line explains) the conclusion of the NBA Finals.)

The National Basketball Association and the National Hockey League both just recently wrapped up their respective seasons. For the NBA, it was probably the best year in the last 15, with a solid regular season exploding into a star-studded playoffs loaded with intrigue, transformational moments, and memorable games. The league garnered its best ratings since the Michael Jordan era, and after six down-to-the-wire NBA Finals games, we all celebrated as "The Good Guys" triumphed over evil, i.e. LeBron James and the Miami Heat. It was truly something to behold, and probably the best all-around playoffs the league has had since I can remember.

The NHL playoffs might've been good as well; I'm not sure. I don't watch hockey.

I was going to write about LeBron here, but since every living soul on the planet beat me to it, it seems a bit pointless. Instead, I'd like to discuss the dynamic between these two leagues.

Some quick background for non-sports fans: in America, there is a hierarchy of sorts among professional sports leagues, mostly based on popularity. Number one with a bullet is the NFL – football is king, plain and simple. It is the most-watched, most talked-about, and generally most-beloved of all pro sports. Advertisers pay millions of dollars for mere seconds of commercial time during the Super Bowl. It's all gotten a little out of hand.

Behind the NFL are the NBA and Major League Baseball, though nobody seems exactly sure of the order. But it doesn't really matter – both leagues are wildly popular and enjoy considerable monetary success. Along with the NFL, these sports are probably the most interwoven in the fabric of American culture. Baseball, basketball, and football are games most young boys play while growing up, and thus the majority of men can relate to at least one of them. Their season's overlap slightly but not enough to create serious conflict, and this allows our attention to casually flow from one into the next. It's a pretty neat and tidy system.

Next in line, and the fourth most popular pro sport in America, is the National Hockey League (unless you count NASCAR, but no rational human being does). Coupled with the aforementioned leagues, it creates what is referred to as "The Big Four" in American sports. But as much as football has a firm grasp on number one, hockey is just as cemented in number four status. Now, the NHL is certainly a prominent league – it's seen a surge in popularity in the last decade, many of the games are televised (at least locally), and its highlights are shown on SportsCenter – but not quite on par with the NFL, NBA, and MLB. For example, you'll often see NHL playoff games on NBC Sports Network, a network that not long ago got most of its programming from deer hunting shows. While respectable, hockey is, at this point, a niche sport.

QUITTING COLD STONE (AND OTHER STRUGGLES)

And really, nobody debates this. Even the most hardcore NHL fan will concede that his or her sport is a distant fourth in the pecking order. And this could be the cause of their issues.

NHL fans are a funny lot. For whatever reason, nearly every one I've ever met seems legitimately offended by the NBA; just pissed off it even exists. I'm pretty sure it's limited to basketball – I haven't come across one that extends this scorn to the NFL or MLB – but it is some serious, deep-rooted hate. I suppose it's due in part to the fact that basketball and hockey seasons more or less mirror each other, and these disgruntled fans feel slighted that the NBA gets all the national attention. A classic big brother/little brother situation seems to be the case here. But these people are not content with just disliking the NBA, they are bound and determined to make sure everyone knows it. It's as if each one has to wage a personal crusade against professional basketball. Anytime the subject comes up in conversation or a game flashes across a TV, they'll mumble a vague insult before starting the spiel. "Fuck," it usually starts, "I hate the fucking NBA." I used to ask them to elaborate, but revealing myself as an NBA sympathizer tends to get the scorn turned on me. Indeed, it seems the fact that I like the NBA offends them even more than the league itself. "How can you watch this shit?" they'll ask with a puckered face, as if the man at an adjacent table just released a string of nauseating chili cheese dog farts. I disgust them. When the urge to punch me in the face subsides, the NHL fan will rattle off his or her personal list of why the NBA is Satan's work:

- **It's a bunch of coddled athletes.** Totally true, but so it is with every major sport. You might as well get over it, unless you plan on turning against the NFL, MLB, and NHL, along with mixed martial arts, boxing, golf, tennis, and European soccer.
- **They don't play defense.** Untrue. This is one of

those ideas that was originally formed some 20 years ago, and contemporary fans lazily use as a crutch when trying to discredit pro basketball. It's kind of like the fax machine – almost completely worthless and impractical, yet every now and then some guy still uses one, so they persist. I get the feeling nobody who says this has actually watched an NBA game in the past three years. Sorry if they're not crouched down in a teeth-gritted defensive stance every second they're on that end of the floor; given this logic, I assume you expect every NFL player to be in a full sprint at all times and every hockey player to never glide on their skates.

- **The players flop to get foul calls.** Absolutely true. I have no defense for this one.

- **The league is made up of ex-convicts.** Quick, off the top of your head, name five current NBA players with criminal records. No? Didn't think so.

- **They don't play hard until the playoffs.** Yes, things get more intense in the postseason, but is there any league where the competition doesn't ramp up a notch in the playoffs?

Anyway, I digress. This isn't about searching for validation for the NBA, because there's really no need for that. As I mentioned earlier, despite my Minnesota roots, I am not a hockey fan. I was raised in a basketball household – Jerry Neumann was a point guard for Winsted Holy Trinity after all, not a right winger – and I just never really got into the sport of hockey. And you know what? That's okay! NBA fans, like most clear-thinking individuals, seem to have a better grasp on the concept of personal choice. We understand that our sport might not be your cup of tea, and we accept that. We will not kick and scream and bitch and moan every time someone brings up the NHL, even if we don't particularly enjoy watching that league, because we understand that your personal tastes might be different from ours. And to quote an oft-used line, we're doing just fine without you.

In the end, no amount of protests, temper tantrums, or face punches is going to change someone's personal preference anyway. People like what they like, and as long as it's not kidnapping or murder, shouldn't we be okay with that? Shouldn't we celebrate diversity in thought? Isn't that what America is about?

These are generally the points I'll bring up if the situation calls for it, but to be honest, more often than not I'm met with blank stares or snide comments. I guess some people just have an issue with the whole "live and let live" thing. Sigh. As my final effort, I might kindly inform the angry party that his or her television is most likely equipped with a remote control, a fabulous device that has the capability to change the channel, and if they are unhappy with what is on their TV screen, they should quietly utilize that function, quit bitching, and call a therapist. Because if you get that bent out of shape about a few guys throwing around an orange ball, you have much bigger issues.

CONFESSIONS OF A WI-FI THIEF

At the time of this writing, it is the year 2012 and I am 25 years old. I live in Boulder, Colorado, a progressive bastion of technology and early adoption, and work in the digital media industry. I am surrounded by solar panels, centers for space and atmospheric exploration, and millions of fiber optic cables running underground, connecting one high tech video system to another.

And I do not own a smartphone.

I give you this unnecessary setup and seemingly pointless punch line only to illustrate the disconnect my personal cellular situation has with the world that surrounds it. Because of my point in history and current location, I can't walk 10 damn feet without being confronted with an iPhone. Seriously, they're everywhere; from adult coworkers to college students to 13 year-old kids at the bus stop, nobody seems to want to fathom a life without Apple's now-flagship device. To a man, it seems like every single person I've met in the last year has an iPhone in their front pocket, ready to text me a photo they took with its glorious 8-megapixel camera. Except my phone doesn't get picture messages.

The last three phones I've bought have been from EBay, years apart, and all cost under $40 (shipping included). Each purchase was only a matter of necessity, due to some sort of malfunction in my previous model. They all are made by companies whose names conjure up memories of simpler times – before data plans and mobile video and GPS – and are equipped with only the most basic features. Text messaging is as advanced as I get.

I do not want a new phone, and will only entertain the notion when my current device inevitably stops working. And then, it's back to the EBay well for more antiquated technology.

The reason for this is not as pompous as it may seem. I will not go on a lengthy diatribe about the perils of modern technology or the interpersonal divide created from the distractions caused by our devices. I have no problem with technology. I am just cheap.

For some reason, I'm the only person on the face of God's great earth that thinks $100 a month is too much to pay for cell service. Yes, there are plenty of different monthly options out there, but with the normal call/text coverage plus the now-mandatory "data plan" for these devices, most of them shake out to be damn near three figures when all is said and done. And that just seems ridiculous to me; I can just think of a thousand things I'd rather spend that money on. Food, gasoline, chocolate bars, prostitu...well, um, the specific things are not important. But for most people I know, their precious iMoneyHole would be the *last* thing they would cut. I know people that are buried in credit card debt or can hardly pay their rent, but there they are, checking Facebook on the ol' smartphone while driving. It's as if the thought of paring that bill from the budget never occurred to them, or maybe the thought of life without an iPhone and unlimited data is so horrific they simply block it out.

Whatever the reason, the iPhone (and other smartphones, to some degree) is and has always been a status symbol, though it's moved from one of luxury to one of necessity. What was once, "oh cool, you have an iPhone?" is now "um, what? You *don't* have an iPhone?" accompanied by a shit-sniffing look of disgust. We non-smartphone users are now the leper outcasts of modern society.

I thoroughly enjoy this minimalist approach and plan to continue, but it does create some unique challenges. Namely: getting internet. Now, as a somewhat connected young adult living and working in a very connected world, going a lengthy amount of time without internet access is simply not an option. Gone are the days of going on vacation and completely turning everything off for the duration of the trip, or even neglecting the email inbox for a full weekend – at least in my line of work. I need to at least feign some semblance of connectivity to the outside world at all times, otherwise I will probably get fired and die. (See? The technology addiction is even in *my* head. It's hopeless). And hell, sometimes I just *want* to get online; take a look at news, Twitter, or fantasy football lineups. I mean, I'm not a complete caveman. Men have certain needs, and consistent internet is one of them. Don't judge me.

The problem with this is that on my days off, I'm not always around a computer – nor do I want to be, given the fact that I'm constantly staring at them on my days *on*. And this is precisely the problem that smartphones solve: ready internet wherever you are. But as I said before, fuck smartphones.

This is the paradox in which I find myself. And yes, I realize it's partially self-inflicted. Shut up.

The beautiful part here is that there's a way out. A loophole, a workaround, a way to beat the system. As I mentioned, I'm not against technology or anything. I own a laptop and an iPod Touch, which is basically an iPhone without the phone functionality or enormous monthly contract. The one-time cost of such devices has never bothered me; it's the consistent financial beatdown that happens 12 times a year. Basically, I fear commitment. This is where the iPod comes in.

I initially bought this device (refurbished at a reduced price, of course) as a painfully-needed upgrade to my old, barely working iPod Nano. It cost less than $300 and was one of the bigger recreational purchases I've made. I was giddy. The plan was to just use it for music and occasionally play some games on it or something – I really had no idea what the thing could do. But soon after getting into it, I learned that it has almost the exact same internet functionality as the iPhone; same mobile browser, same apps, even the same messaging system. The only thing it lacks is the 3g or 4g network functionality, which is fine, because that's what requires ~~an anal pounding~~ a contract. Instead, it uses Wi-Fi.

Now my path to the internet only had a single barrier: Wi-Fi. And the great thing about the tech boom of the 21st Century? Wi-Fi is virtually everywhere. I don't quite understand it, given that most people have 3g connectivity on their smartphone and don't actually *need* wireless internet, but businesses and places of leisure seem to feel obligated to provide it most of the time. So pretty much wherever I am, I can live the smartphone lifestyle without the smartphone contract.

Of course, free wireless internet isn't *everywhere*, and it's not always easily accessible. This leads to what I call "the Chase;" my daily struggle to find Wi-Fi when I need (or want) to get online. A few places can be ruled out right off the bat: the car and nature. Obviously I'm not going to find a wireless network while driving down the freeway or walking through the woods, so there's no real reason to try. But pretty much everywhere else is in play; bars, restaurants, college campuses, apartment buildings, retail stores, even church. If I'm at or near one of these places for a prolonged period of time, the Chase begins.

Sometimes it's easy – many establishments will intentionally leave wireless networks unsecured for customer use, those compassionate souls. I love these places. But sometimes it's harder – there's no network explicitly provided for customers or passers-by, and I have to get creative. So I employ some learned techniques, such as:

- Refreshing the list of available networks on my device a few times. Often times weaker signals won't get picked up the first time, but will show up and be available for connection after a few tries. These are generally pretty slow if they work at all, but hey, moochers can't be choosers.

- Moving my location. Often times, even going from one end of the room to another will pick up a new network from nearby.

- Looking for networks named Linksys or D-Link or other words that sound like a brand of generic wireless router. These are a dead giveaway of wireless gold; usually when a wireless network is set up, the default network name will be that of the router brand. And if whoever sets it up doesn't know how to change the network name, they sure as hell don't know how to make it password protected. Unsecured. Jackpot.

- If the only networks available are password protected, I'll arbitrarily guess passwords based on the network name. This one doesn't have a very high success rate.

Almost wherever I am, there's at least a chance I can find free Wi-Fi. Some places give it out like condoms at college orientation, and thus gain preferred status from me. We'll call them "Platinum" members. Others put it under lock and key and charge up the ass, and suck the life out of the world. They get a "Brown" ranking, for poop, of course. A quick breakdown of the spectrum:

Providers of Wi-Fi and Their Rankings

Platinum: Starbucks and most other coffee shops (the shining examples of wireless generosity), libraries, Panera Bread, the Kansas City Airport, the guy that lives next door to my girlfriend (network name: DLink).

Gold: Most fast food restaurants (they finally seem to be catching on), bars on NFL Sundays, college campuses (usually available but often has hoops to jump through).

Gray: Sit-down restaurants, bars NOT on NFL Sundays, hotel lobbies, most apartment buildings, all airports not located in Kansas City.

Brown: Hotel rooms (These are truly the worst. I cannot remember a time when I stayed at a hotel that provided free Wi-Fi in the rooms, or even a remote opportunity to mooch from somewhere else. And if you really *do* need to get online, so much you're willing to (GASP!) actually pay for it, a credit card sodomization is sure to occur. Ridiculous rates like $10-$15 a day are commonplace. They have certainly earned a Brown rating).

This is of course not an exhaustive list, but a snapshot of some more popular establishments with Wi-Fi. Feel free to add your own to the list – I don't mind. It's for the good of the land.

Recently I will admit to straying a bit and considering the idea of a smartphone. The Chase had worn me down a bit I suppose, and I went as far as researching data plans and iPhone pricing. *Maybe I should just do it*, I thought to myself. *Everyone else has one, and it definitely would be more convenient. Perhaps it's time.* I even crunched the numbers and made the outlandish monthly plan work with my budget – a smartphone was, for the first time, a possibility for me if I so chose.

But then I knew, in my heart of hearts, I couldn't do it. I could not give up fighting the good fight and simply pay the piper. It would be giving in, but I didn't care about that

– no, what I realized is that I would miss the Chase. Hours spent combing the airwaves for a sliver of a sign, that glorious rush of achievement when I saw that little blue check mark confirming I was connected to a network I probably wasn't supposed to be using, the triumphant checking of Facebook and reworking of fantasy football lineups on someone else's dime...none of this would be necessary anymore. I would simply bust out my phone and go straight to the internet – there would be no challenge. And I would be dead inside.

I'm sure someday I'll be forced to get a smartphone – hey, if a third party (such as an employer) is for some reason willing to purchase the phone *and* pay for the monthly plan, I would totally be on board. But right now, I just can't bring myself to do it. I would miss the Chase.

One-Year Later Update: I am a fraud and the smartphone people have won. It was the parents.

For my last birthday they presented me with a brand new iPhone and offered to add the data package to their already-active family plan. It is reasonably priced, it works wonderfully, I am enjoying it immensely and I feel incredibly dirty.

You see, I am completely and totally under the spell of the machine. It is quite frankly amazing; the iPhone does almost exactly what my iPhone Touch did, but is sleeker, faster, more accessible, and all-around more enjoyable. A few months in, I haven't picked up the iPod since I was blessed with the phone. I always suspected there was a wide world I was missing by not owning a smartphone, but I was afraid to take the plunge, knowing I would never be able to go back. Well, I'm engulfed now, and certainly past the point of no return.

It has sucked me in, and I'm beginning to get as addicted as everyone else. In all sorts of social situations – meetings, gatherings of friends, conversations with my girlfriend – I find myself whipping it out and scrolling through the apps. I don't know what I'm looking for, but it just seems like the right thing to do.

Yes, it has the 4G data connectivity, providing me with internet access almost anywhere. This is of course incredible. But sometimes, just sometimes, I do one little thing to stay true to my roots.

In a bar, restaurant, or foreign apartment building, I will break from whatever group I'm in and find cover in a corner somewhere. There, I'll bust out the iPhone and go to the Settings page, where I'll work meticulously like the old pro I am at finding an unsecured wireless network. It's unnecessary, it makes little sense, but it makes me feel alive. And smartphone or not, that's all anyone can ask.

FOIE GRAS REDUCTION

Course One – House made Scrapple with Fennel Kimchi & Creamy Shallot Confit Barley

Course Two – Barley & Quinoa "Risotto" with Winter Vegetables, Crispy Poached Egg, and Basil & Preserved Orange Pistou

Above are dining options from a restaurant I'll be visiting later this week. It's been my experience over the course of my life that restaurants generally serve food, but after reading this I'm not so sure. I assume it's food – I do notice certain familiar terms like "egg" and "vegetables" in there – but with so many colorfully misleading and probably made-up words in the description, I certainly don't want to bank on that. For instance, I thought barley is what they fed the horses on my uncle's farm. Perhaps this restaurant is for livestock. Others such as "scrapple" and "quinoa" confuse me to no end; the former sounds like a genre of steel guitar music from the fifties. And I find it particularly worrisome that there are quotes around the word "risotto." That is one word I was beginning to feel comfortable with, but now my guard is back up. Why the quotes? It's as if they're saying it with a wink and nod, and we're expected to be in on the joke. Well I am certainly not in on the joke, for I have no idea what the hell they mean, and I'd appreciate a more straightforward, quote-free description in the future.

Slightly dramatic embellishments aside, this is clearly not a menu from Outback Steakhouse. It's restaurant week in Denver; that time of year when even the outlandishly expensive restaurants are reasonably priced and diners are encouraged to get out and eat. Actually spanning two weeks, restaurant "week" is a great time to be human, as the low prices and abundant options make a great opportunity to try something new. And to that end, the Denver/Boulder area is a blessed place for food-lovers to be in general, with a wide variety of top-notch eateries mostly focused on quality and freshness of ingredients and healthy experimentation. And who among us doesn't love food?

But there comes a time and place when the love for food is taken too far and the experimentation gets unhealthy. The white plates get bigger, and the food in the middle gets smaller. The menu at the top is an example of this – it's obvious at first glance it's among the snootier places one could find (hell, menu items also include bone marrow and lamb neck), so it's certainly not the norm. But it seems this is becoming more and more mainstream.

Now, I promise you, I'm not *completely* uncultured swine – I do enjoy a good gourmet meal. I can appreciate new foods and culinary creativity, and I don't need every main course to be a steak. I've had my share of large plate/small food meals, and have enjoyed most every one of them. However, sometimes it seems that we get a little caught up in using colorful and "foodie" academic words – "confit," "foie gras," and "reduction" come to mind – in some attempt at an air of class and exclusivity. I think the food snobs are becoming more numerous, and they care more about being able to name outlandish ingredients than having a truly pleasing meal. And maybe, just maybe, some chefs are more concerned with impressing other chefs and with how a dish looks (and sounds on the menu), than how a dish tastes. It's as if the more times you can work "crusted" and "gnocchi" and "butternut" and "crème fraiche" on a menu, the more status you have among food snobs.

Personally, I just want to have a tasty meal, and I don't want to have to learn another fucking language to order it. If I have to try to decipher what "aioli" is one more time, I may just stab the pompous ass waiting on us with a fork. It's not his fault, of course, but his thick-framed glasses and neck beard just fit him right into the food snob stereotype.

What if we treated other areas of life the same way we treat food? For example:

Al Michaels calling a football game

The call: "Peterson takes the handoff, runs right and picks up six yards."

The foodie version: "The distinguished man of Texan descent is delivered the dried cow membrane, harnesses its energy and grasps its succulence. The run is the antithesis of to the left, with plastic cleat spears juxtaposed against Floridian sod and topsoil, moving the main course from its origin to six yards beyond. Yardage reduction."

Christmas Store Ad

The ad: "Christmas time is coming! You'd better get your shopping done."

The foodie version: "The sparkling anniversary of the first Noel, when Jesus "Yahweh" Christ descended upon the Israeli region, has again been assumed to happen this 25th of Diciembre as previously scheduled. Imperative, it is, that the customers finish his or her retail extravaganza in a timely fashion, before the inevitable human flooding of cement and granite structures makes such an endeavor burdensome, and the sterling prospect of yuletide cheer transforms into a substandard procession."

Clothing tag
The tag: "100% cotton"
The foodie version: "Pure, unadulterated, locally farm-raised *algadon*. Never synthetic, never poly, a classic "hand-weave" with light ulterior stitching and authentic Mandarin craftsmanship."

See? It's ridiculous. If we were all as pretentious as the food snobs, our lives would be a constant exercise in trying to decipher even the simplest of labels. I'm sure I'll enjoy my parsnip meringue – or whatever they decide to serve this week – but that doesn't mean I won't make an effort to fart each time I walk near the kitchen, just to bring the uppity vibe in there a notch closer to reality. I wonder how they'd describe *that*?

FIVE THOUGHTS ON JOHN MAYER

1. He's the best guitarist in pop music (as of early 2013).
...and has been for the better part of a decade. This is of course impossible to prove, and I suspect half those reading it will immediately jump to disagreement and loudly exclaim a name or three who are obviously *far* superior to Mayer as guitarists (music dorks, self included, love to argue), and the other half are like most pop music listeners and don't give a damn about guitar playing. Very well then.

Guitar playing is a matter of personal preference, and while we can all generally agree on discernible levels of skill, one man's Lenny Kravitz is another's Tommy Emmanuel. Confused? Me too. But basically what I'm saying is, "diff'rent strokes for different folks," and for my money, it doesn't (currently) get better than when John Mayer decides to unload on his Strat. You can get an idea of what I mean from searching YouTube for live performances of "Wait Till Tomorrow" or "Gravity," but basically I think when Mayer decides he's going to let loose and bust a solo – and that's a big "when" – he's the closest thing we have to Hendrix, Page, et al.

Admittedly, I put a lot of stock in soloing. Probably too much. I do understand and appreciate the merits of quality chord voicings, progressions, and strumming patterns. But to me, the solo is where the true beauty of the music comes through, where an artist can stop thinking and planning and let his (or her) soul take over. Stevie Ray Vaughan once said that if you play a single note with soul and feeling, it will be better than a thousand notes sprayed across the fretboard with skill and acumen, but without real emotion behind it. Stevie knew what he was talking about. I liken it to football: rudimentary chord strumming and riffing is like a running back running up the middle for a four or five yard gain; it's effective and often a winning formula, but it lacks a certain panache. Conversely, the solo is when the back breaks free into the open field, hurdling over and spinning around would-be tacklers, and flailing with reckless abandon. This is where the true beauty of the game lies, and while the former is necessary, the latter is why we watch. And John Mayer is Adrian Peterson.

Whether you agree with me or not, you must (i.e. I am forcing you to) agree that John Mayer can lay down a blues solo *at least* as good as any other current artist on the market. I hear cries of Dan Auerbach of the Black Keys and Jack White all the time, and while I deeply appreciate both musicians – and their respective guitar stylings – neither can hold a candle to John Mayer when it comes to improvisation. I certainly would like it if they could, because I respect their total body of work more than I do his. But they can't.

Don't believe me? Look up some of his live sets– anything from his "Where the Light Is" show or the Crossroads festivals in Chicago will do. Just sit back and listen, and when the song builds into Mayer's inevitably tone-perfect tear, the only way your arm hair *won't* stand up is if you have no soul or you listen to Bruno Mars (and I have a suspicion the two things might be connected). He is an absolute master of the fretboard, a man who can play (and has played) right along with a lot of blues legends. This trait of his is understandably lost on most of the listening public, due to the fact that the only Mayer tunes that make the radio are his acoustic sap-fests.

Which is totally soulless, terrible, and wrong, and leads to the next item...

2. Most of his albums are borderline unlistenable.

For a guy that claims Stevie Ray Vaughan and Jimi Hendrix as major influences, John Mayer sure does write a lot of quiet, effeminate songs for the girls. And there's absolutely nothing *wrong* with those types of songs, if that's your thing. If you're into that stuff, fine, but you have *so many* artists to enjoy. The music world is teeming with teeny-bopper love tunes, so can't you just let me have THIS ONE THING?!

I'm sorry, I overreacted. It's not your fault, it's his. Over the course of his career, John Mayer has proven that that type of music *is* his thing. I just think it's a damn shame, because he can do so much better.

Look, I'm not saying acoustic, radio-friendly love songs are a dime a dozen, but they're no more expensive than ten for a dollar. And the transcendence of Mayer's electric guitar is priceless, so much that I don't understand why he doesn't use it more. Nobody can do what he can, not in this decade anyway.

Growing up, John Mayer was so obsessed with playing the guitar that his parents took him to see a psychiatrist twice. His singular focus was that alarming. He was deemed mentally sound, just introverted and weirdly obsessed, so much that after high school he worked 15 months at a gas station just to make enough money to buy a Stevie Ray signature Stratocaster. People with these single-minded eccentricities towards guitar playing don't grow up to become chord strummers; they become Eddie Van Halen, Mike McCready, and Jeff Beck. When the guitar is in your blood, you want to do more than just caress the instrument; you want to pound the living shit out of it until it's given you every ounce of tone it has. You want to hammer it until it becomes part of you. And I know it's in Mayer's blood, because I've seen it.

So that's why I don't understand things like *Room for Squares* and *Heavier Things*. Mayer's first two major label albums are the epitome of acoustic pop – singles like "Daughters" and "Your Body is a Wonderland" pretty much sum it up – and in the world of Billboard top charts, were wildly successful. And maybe that's what he wanted – hell, what musician wouldn't want commercial success? Obviously blues guitar doesn't sell nearly as well as "No Such Thing." But after you'd made your first 10 million, and after you're firmly established as a prominent musician, then wouldn't it be time to take a little chance and let that guitar loose a little bit? Who cares if the album undersells (which it inevitably would)? You already won.

Part of my frustration comes from the fact that he's teased us with this very thing on a few occasions. After *Heavier Things*, he declared in an interview he was ready to "close up shop on acoustic sensitivity." What followed was *Continuum*, unquestionably Mayer's finest studio album and a definite step in the right direction. Around the same time, he started touring with bassist Pino Palladino and drummer Steve Jordan as the John Mayer Trio, a power blues outfit that was the embodiment of everything Mayer can do. The group released one live album, *Try!*, and it was of course totally badass and awesome. Sweeping solos and pounding rhythm, all tied together with Mayer's crisp vocals and impeccable timing, it wasn't just a jam record but a tight, shining example of what modern blues could be.

Then Mayer began working on his next album, to be

called *Battle Studies*, and informed us that he'd be recording with his Trio bandmates (who had also played on *Continuum*). Also, he said through interviews and press releases, he would be going in *another* new direction.

I was so damn excited. Clearly the time has come, I thought, and he's realized he's ready to be done with all that soft shit and give us a balls-to-the-wall, bitchin' blues album. I could. Not. Wait.

The result? The album sucked. Of course it did. I was crushed. *Battle Studies* ended up being more *Heavier Things* than *Try!*, as the power and majesty from the Trio's live performances were nonexistent on the record. The initial single "Who Says" was fun and catchy (if subdued), but others such as "Heartbreak Warfare" and "Half of My Heart" were just as cheesy as their names indicate. Even Mayer's cover of "Crossroads" disappointed; it severely lacked the punch Mayer is able to capture live. It was back to the drawing board for me.

Maybe it's a studio vs. live thing. Most live concerts are able to up the energy over their album counterparts, and thus are often more enjoyable. But the gap in John Mayer's work is so big it's astounding. It's like he's not even trying to bring that live feel into the studio. And maybe he isn't.

3. He WILL stand the test of time.

Despite all of this, the guy is a really damn good musician. And not just the guitar skills, either; Mayer has a quality voice, a knack for songwriting, and an obvious musical charm to which people gravitate.

My friends and I like to kick around the idea of which musicians from our generation will still be relevant in 30 years. With so many forgettable acts –Nicki Minaj, Three Days Grace, something called Ke$ha...I could go on – getting the majority of the play, it often seems like the answer is "none of them." With the benefit of hindsight, we look back at the sixties and seventies, and bands like Led Zeppelin, the Rolling Stones, and the Beatles, and it seems obvious that they would still be played decades later. These are transcendent bands that helped shape rock and roll history. But did the listeners know that at the time? Was it obvious that certain bands would stand the test of time, or is that a realization that can only happen when given historical context?

I would guess the latter, and that keeps me hopeful that there will be a handful of musicians from the turn-of-the-century period that still matter in the distant future. And I think John Mayer has as good a shot as any. He touches enough demographics but hasn't been completely played out.

Even in the face of my overarching claim that Mayer's studio work is subpar, the one glaring exception is *Continuum*. It is, by any definition, a superb album. It is overall a slow record with some of Mayer's trademark vaginal traits, but that is only problematic when considering my own personal bias, and by itself says nothing about quality. *Continuum* starts with its top single, "Waiting on the World to Change," a quasi-protest song that's part Jason Mraz and part Marvin Gaye. It's serviceable. But as the album rambles on, Mayer stops trying and starts being himself, and things get good. "Gravity," "Slow Dancing in a Burning Room," and "Dreaming with a Broken Heart" are uniformly fantastic tracks that finally find the happy medium between Mayer's earlier album work and his formidable stage presence; medium-tempo, watery vocals supported by an almost always prominent guitar lick and a rock solid (yet restrained) rhythm section. And hey, there's even a guitar solo every now and then! What a concept. John even feels more like himself when he's being someone else; his cover of Hendrix's "Bold as Love" is fairly strong and comes as close to doing the song justice as any mere mortal can. Just having the balls to cover Jimi is impressive, and doing it reasonably well is grounds for an award.

The album finishes with "I'm Gonna Find Another

You," a jazzy breakup tune that's allegedly about Jennifer Aniston or some other famous blonde. It's a great, semi-anthemic cap on the record, and showcases Mayer's unique talents better than any other track on any other album. Bringing the boys and girls together is not an easy task, and John pulls it off.

Continuum feels comfortable, like what John Mayer wants to play, what he's *supposed* to play. The man has soul, and it pours out in the record. He's still at his best live, but I have a feeling we'll be hearing cuts of *Continuum* long after Mayer hangs it up.

4. He's probably a tool.

This is evident to most, based on his public womanizing, comments such as "with great power comes great responsibility" (regarding his musical talent), and the fact that he's John Mayer. As common folk with no real connection to the man whatsoever, we can never truly know what kind of person he is. He is a celebrity, and all we can do is view his life through media and tabloids, which is no way to judge a man's character. But all signs point to douche.

To illustrate this point, I humbly present to you an interaction my girlfriend randomly had with John Mayer back in the day:

Once upon a time, there was a buxom young blonde coming of age in Connecticut. We'll call her Kristen, because that's her name. (Shit, did I do that wrong?). This is long before I ever knew the lass, and just after John Mayer had found his first – if limited – fame with *Room for Squares* and that "I wanna run through the halls of my high school" song. Kristen, in her early 20s, was at her apartment getting ready for a Saturday night out. She was going out with her older sister to a party consisting mostly of the sister's friends, which was generally a good time; the sis knew how to party. So Kristen prepared the way every woman does: by spending far too much time worrying about what she would wear.

Tonight, there was one accessory in particular that was giving her fits: a belt. It was a large, somewhat gaudy take on the traditional belt, with leather tassels hanging off of it. Kristen liked it – found it very "cute," as it were – but wondered if it was too much. There is a baseline level of risks one can reasonably take with clothing; approach the line without going over and look fabulous, but go too far and look like a fool. She stood in front of the mirror and held the belt up to her waist, then took it away, repeating five or six times. Yay or nay, she wondered. Yay or nay?

To hell with it, Kristen decided, she was wearing the belt. It was cute.

She shows up at sis' house in Norwalk, Conn., where the party was being held. It was a good sized, two-level operation, with bars set up both upstairs and downstairs. They mingle for a while downstairs and notice a palpable buzz – more than just your standard Saturday night buzz. The place was pretty full. Big sis did some investigation and soon returned with this nugget: John Mayer was there.

Yes, the mop-haired heartthrob was roaming the house somewhere, and the women in the place could not be more smitten. Kristen found this interesting and relatively exciting, but she was able to refrain from dropping her beverage and running around screaming. She would go about her business, and if she saw him, she saw him.

And before long, that's what happened. Kristen ventured upstairs alone to get a drink, and as she finished ascending the stairs, there he was – leaning on the bar by himself in his leather jacket.

She was flustered. The man himself was right there, standing...alone! Kristen instantly knew she must talk to him. But how? Surely she couldn't just approach the guy – he was John F'ing Mayer. So she did what many twenty-something do in such situations: she began pounding drinks to work up the courage.

Luckily there were enough people mingling upstairs to

provide a buffer. She approached the other end of the bar and got her first vodka-soda, and soon it was down the hatch. Then another, and before long she lost count. Her head became foggy, her inhibitions loosened, and approaching John Mayer began to seem like more and more of a possibility. One more beverage, she decided, and then she would be ready to go.

Then he appeared beside her and spoke.

"I really like your belt."

Holy shit, was he talking to her? Surely he was – nobody else could be wearing such a bitchin' accessory. Sweet validation! Kristen turned his direction, and sure enough, John Mayer was leaning on the bar, facing her, and addressing her belt.

"Oh," she swooned, "I mean, thank you." And then, she felt compelled to go on. "You know, I want to say, I think you're a great musician. I'm not trying to be corny or anything, but I just really appreciate your music." It was an honest sentiment, if a little fangirl-ish.

"Well in a way, that's ironic," he said, "because where as your belt is meant to hold your pants up, my music is meant to take women's pants down."

She blushed, mumbled something incoherent, and turned and walked away. She honestly didn't know what else to do. Did John Mayer just hit on her?

Whether or not he did, I don't really care. But who *says* that? "My music is meant to take women's pants down." How is that not the embodiment of the douchebag musician? It's an isolated incident...and it's also true...but it's basically credible evidence that directly supports my entire John Mayer theory; he chooses to (for the most part) neglect his real talent and instead focus on subdued pop rock in order to a) have sex with women, and b) harness the record-buying force that is teenage girls (and their parents). This is his end goal, to make money and get laid. Which certainly doesn't make him unique among famous pop artists, but does make him harder to appreciate from a strictly artistic standpoint.

5. He's probably a genius.

At the time I write this, John has just recently released *Born and Raised*, his fifth studio album. It is a notable shift from his previous work. *Born and Raised* ventures into a folky, Western, Crosby, Stills, and Nash (and sometimes Young) territory. The transition was probably born initially from his infamous *Playboy* interview, when he essentially made a total ass of himself in front of the entire nation. If you haven't heard of it (i.e. don't read *Playboy* or gossip columns), check it out – it's pretty alarming, and totally supports Thought #4. The interview and subsequent backlash was an apparent eye-opener, so he withdrew from the public eye for two years, moved to Montana, grew long hair and a feeble mustache, and began wearing large hats. Somewhere in there he wrote and recorded *Born and Raised*.

Given the circumstances, the record is about half of what you'd expect; Americana twang with enough pop to be a John Mayer album, but it sounds oddly...happy. Not dark and brooding like you often hear from something made in withdrawal and seclusion, but for the most part bright and upbeat, as if he's literally "headed out west with [his] headphones on" like he sings in the opening track.

And the album is actually pretty cool. Despite it not being what I keep asking for, it's an honest, respectable recording. Perhaps the "real" John Mayer that I lionize in my mind is not actually who the real John Mayer is; perhaps this is him, or maybe he will show up three or four records down the road. But what's important is that *Born and Raised* feels like Mayer taking a step towards finding the real him, even if he doesn't know who that actually is yet (or if he ever will).

Which is where the word "genius" comes in. We often think of a genius as someone all-knowing and nearly omnipotent – someone who has it all figured out and is just waiting on the rest of us to catch up. But I don't think that's it, at least not in music. True genius in art is recognizing you *aren't* all-knowing and you *don't* have it all figured out, but possessing a constant drive to learn as much as you can through your work. Being dedicated to a constant chase of perfection, while knowing fully its achievement is never possible.

Albums like *Born and Raised*, *Continuum*, and *Try!* show that pursuit. John Mayer's music is constantly evolving, not in a clichéd Metallica sort of way, but based on the reality that on each album he's introduced different sounds and concepts, and approached the entire process in a unique way. The result isn't always devout excellence, but it has far more value than an artist who recognizes a successful formula and never strays from it. Early on, I thought this was who John Mayer was. But I was wrong. He's an artist that's in a constant search of himself, and whether or not he'll ever find it, I'm not sure. But it'll be a hell of a trip when it's all said and done.

ODE TO AUDI

Do not be fooled by the advertisements. They are lies.

All of that stuff about German engineering? Horseshit. The smartest car on the road? More like the dumbest kid in school. Best in class this, best value that, highest rated something...you're talking, but all I'm hearing is "blah...blah...blah."

Of course I'm talking about you, Audi. You and your bullshit marketing campaigns, your snake-oil products and features, and your smug citations of awards and high ratings. You are either deliberately spreading falsehoods or simply delirious, for the only way you are the "best value" in anything is if the car owners "value" having a proverbial stick shoved up their asses once every few months. You are the worst, and I will tell you why.

I've been the proud owner of one of your lauded (German Engineered!!!) vehicles for some five years now, and the experience has been nothing but one gigantic aneurysm. I'm fairly confident that I and a class of preschoolers could engineer a machine that would hold up better, and none of us are even German.

Oh, it started out swell. I was seduced by your charm,

you slick bastard, when I bought the car at 48,000 miles. The supple leather, the sleek interior, the immaculate paint and trim – for a used car, I felt I had done pretty damn well. It was choice. My friends commented on how good it looked, how well it rode, how the engine purred, and I nodded along. They were impressed, and I was happy.

One day while admiring the fine machine, a friend's dad asked casually how much I knew about Audi's.

"Well," I admitted, "not a whole lot. But they seem like nice cars."

He – in as nice a way as possible – gave me the book on Audi, and none of it was good. "From what I see, they just seem to have a lot of problems after they hit 50,000 miles. You might be just fine, but I usually try to advise people against buying them if possible. If the sale isn't final yet, you actually might want to reconsider."

I dismissed it as hogwash. I would be fine; I had German engineering on my side. Besides, the sale was final.

And for a while, I *was* fine. Things were great, actually – no issues for the first few months, and the thing ran like a damn spaceship. I did nothing but treat it well and love it; washed it once a week, waxed the shit out of it each summer, treated the leather with fine creams and kept the dash spotless and Armor All-ed. I loved it, and it loved me back. We were smitten. What a fool that man must've been.

Then it began. At first the clutch went, then the cruise control, then all four brake rotors. That was the first year. After that, it basically turned into a constant, suffocating avalanche of malfunctions and deteriorated parts, many of which I cannot pronounce and didn't know existed. I would get one problem fixed, drive the pitiful machine for six months, be lulled into a state of false confidence, and then three new problems would surface. It was maddening. And let's not forget, aside from the sheer volume of work that needed to be done, all of Audi's top quality

German engineered parts cost at least three times as much as those of a normal, practical, working car. I could subsidize all the farms of the third world with the money I've put into this godforsaken automobile.

At current time, I'm a week removed from spending another $50,000 (quite possibly an embellishment, but not by as much as you'd think) to fix the third major alignment problem in the past two years. I've literally rebuilt most of the underbody at this point. And just yesterday, when I walked to my car before work, I noticed a spot under the engine. There is coolant leaking. Fabulous! A quick Google search of the issue indicates that it is most likely either a minor (in the neighborhood of $100) fix, or a much more serious one, to the tune of about $1000. You and I both know damn well which one it will be. It is NEVER the minor problem. I don't believe the German language has a word for "minor." And when fixing this major issue, it's a dead-set lock that something else will surface as well. "

Well," the mechanic will say, as he always does, "once we got in there, we also found your left front radiator crankshaft router was cracked, so we're gonna need to replace that, otherwise the car will spontaneously combust the next time you get in it. I'd also recommend we fix the rest of the radiator crankshaft routers – there are 19 – because they're about a month away from having the same problem. The total comes to $26,748, before tax."

This is fine, of course. Who really needs to pay rent or eat?

I can hear your rebuttal now, Audi, so just shut up. I already know what you're going to say. *Sam, your car is 15 years old. What do you expect?* Well, I guess one expectation would be not having to pay the equivalent of the average person's student loan debt in repairs over the life of the car. That seems somewhat reasonable. And while I understand the age thing, the car only has 110,000 miles on it. Up there, yes, but certainly shouldn't be in take-out-a-second-mortgage-on-your-home-to-keep-this-thing-running territory. I've seen many vehicles easily make it to 200,000, without the need for constant extravagant repairs, and – amazingly – without the aid of German engineering. It's clearly not that hard, except for you Audi, you worthless whore.

Well Sam, maybe you just got a lemon. With the millions of cars we produce, there are bound to be a few defects. We all make mistakes, can you forgive us? Not a chance in hell, for this is bullshit. My car is certainly the worst, but nearly everyone I know who's owned an Audi shares the frustration. A coworker had an extremely expensive "engine sludge" issue – for which there was a class-action lawsuit, by the way – which he would've had to pay for out of pocket if he hadn't been able to prove he'd serviced it regularly (and thus was covered by the settlement). My girlfriend owns a newer version of my car, and has had a laundry list of things break. Both of her rear windows are currently being held up by old concert pamphlets jammed in the window base, for they are non-working and off the tracks. She refuses to get them fixed, and I don't blame her.

Alright Sam, it's clear this hasn't worked for us. We're sorry. Why don't you just sell the car, get what you can, and buy a new car? First of all, apology not accepted. Second, despite the money I've had to dump into this spawn of Satan, it still breaks down to less than a car payment, which – after dumping said money – I certainly can't take on now. Also, I fear the commitment, which is why I bought a (gently) used car in the first place. And really, get what I can for it? How much am I really going to get for a 15 year-old car with no a/c and no cruise control? What's my sales pitch going to be? "Oh, I've already fixed pretty much everything that could possibly go wrong. There's nothing left on this car to fix"? That should work as well as a Brett Favre picture message.

Audi, you are the reason I drink. I hate you and everything you stand for. As soon as my transmission breaks – one of the few things I haven't had to pay for yet – I am planning on flying directly to your headquarters in Ingolstadt, Germany and throwing the damn thing through a window, you Bavarian clothes-wearing pricks. If Hitler is actually still alive, he clearly works for you.

WASTING YOUR VOTE

(Written in the months leading up to the 2012 United State Presidential Election.)

"I don't really like either of the candidates this year."
"Are you gonna vote?"
"Yeah. I'll probably just pick the lesser of two evils."
"You know, you could vote third-party. You don't have to just decide between Democrat and Republican."
"I'm not going to waste my vote."

This is a conversation I've had many times – in different permutations – throughout my life. It of course involves an upcoming U.S. presidential election, where (shockingly) neither the Democrat nor the Republican candidate are all that appealing (are they ever?). Yet it's been beaten into us that although there are literally dozens of candidates running, if we don't vote for one of the big two, our vote is null, wasted, and meaningless.

Why is this?

Let's look at how an election in a constitutional republic – such as ours – works: multiple candidates run for public office. Every competent citizen over the age of 18

QUITTING COLD STONE (AND OTHER STRUGGLES)

without a bunch of felonies has the opportunity to select their preferred candidate, i.e. cast their vote. These votes are tabulated, and whichever candidate garners the most is the winner and takes public office.* (*Sort of. In the U.S., it's not a straight up direct popular vote for presidential office; we employ the "electoral college," a concept that many citizens kind of – but very few completely – understand. It basically attempts to give more power to the individual states, adding up the total vote of each state's populous, then awarding a pre-determined amount of delegates (based on population) to whichever candidate gets the most votes from that state's citizens. Or something. See? I have no idea how it works exactly. But for the most part, whichever candidate gets the most votes nationally usually wins.)

Boring shit aside, for some reason the Democratic and Republican parties seized the lion's share of American political power before any of us were born, and it's just kind of stayed that way. Since 1853, when Franklin Pierce was elected as a Democrat, the office of the president has been in a constant stranglehold by the donkeys and elephants. Yep, presidents 14 through 44 were all a member of one of the big two parties. It's all we know. (Interesting side note: Abe Lincoln, the guy who freed the slaves, was a Republican. Good lord, how things have changed.)

As continuity breeds continuity, this stranglehold has only gotten tighter, to the point where the American people can't seem to fathom a life without either a Democrat or Republican president. It's so ingrained in our minds that the idea of voting for a different party, a "third party" as they're condescendingly referred to, seems like a complete waste of time. They won't win, no matter their ideas or values or political acumen, so we won't vote for them. Because nobody likes standing in a polling line just to throw away their vote, just as nobody likes to side with a loser.

The odd thing is, "we the people" couldn't be unhappier

about the vice grip the big two parties have on the presidency. A Gallup poll from July 2012 revealed that 69% of Americans were dissatisfied with the way "things were going" in the U.S. And that's an improvement – it was the first time since 2009 it was below 70%. Both Democrats and Republicans registered satisfaction ratings below 50% in the poll, with the GOP turning in a truly ungodly rating of 10%. We don't really like any of these guys; we're sick of them, and fed up with the fact that they overpromise, under-deliver, and generally suck at their jobs. It requires no logical leap to peg the American people ready for a change. Yet we refuse to vote for one.

We bitch. We moan. We listen to radio talk shows that rail against the system, and other radio talk shows that rail against those radio talk shows. Some of us choose not to vote, and consider ourselves "apathetic" to the whole notion of politics. The bastards have finally driven us away; it's their fault. We hate them, and all we want is a change – an end to the bickering and in-fighting and heel dragging, and at least some sliver of honesty, compromise, and progress. We pray (or, for Democrats, hope really hard) that something, somehow, can inject some life and sunshine into this godforsaken clusterfuck in Washington.

Well you know what? We can. The clichéd American people. At a very basic level, we run shit around here. Our votes hold the power. It's our house, dammit, and these Washingtonian assholes work for us. We pay their ridiculous salaries. And also, the only way in hell it's going to happen is if we make it happen. Because they have no reason to change.

This isn't some hippie utopian idealism, I promise; it's simple logic. We don't vote for third parties – and thus for REAL change – because we're worried nobody else will, and our vote will be rendered useless. How can we not realize that we are the everyone else? If you chose to vote for the "lesser of two evils" because of this logic, you are the very person that's rendering every potential outside-the-box vote useless. You are the person to whom you're reacting. The only reason we don't vote for third parties is because we're worried people won't vote for third parties. Um, what?

It may sound like I'm advocating voting third party. That's because I am. If you never vote Democrat or Republican again, and stop caring about what the other lemmings do, you'll probably be happy about it; no matter which empty suit is up on that podium fucking up Washington, you'll know it won't be your fault. And if it is – if we somehow miraculously band together and overthrow the vice-grip the Dueling Legions of Esteemed Jackasses has had on the presidency since eighteen fifty fucking three – at least it'll be a new kind of fucked up. At least we won't be perpetuating the definition of insanity.

So which third party candidate should you vote for? I don't care. It honestly doesn't matter, at least in the next lifetime or so. I'm not trying to tell you voting for a third party candidate will get them elected in the near future; it won't. But if you do, you're making an investment in our future. Think of it as a gift to your children (or somebody else's kids, if the idea of procreating scares you as much as it does me), a good-faith effort to make things better for future generations. At this point, you're not voting for the candidate nearly as much as you are the idea – the idea that we don't have to just take what we're given, to accept the lesser of two evils. The insane notion that the citizens of the reigning greatest country in the world actually have a say in our elections.

I suppose it's possible that meaningful and positive change happens through one – or both – of the ruling parties. It could happen, hypothetically, without the need for a third party. Conceivably, a unique and truly charismatic candidate could emerge, galvanizing the country and exciting the people with promises of real and possible hope, change, and general rejection of the status quo. The people would elect him, rejoice in the event, and prosperity and rationalization of the political community would surely follow.

But we've seen that movie before, haven't we?

The single biggest argument for the rogue (third party) vote – the nail in the coffin, at least in my mind – is the 2008 election and subsequent presidency of Barack Obama. It goes to prove without a shadow of a doubt, that if we stick to political parties 1A and 1B, we will always and forever continue to be fucked. This has absolutely nothing to do with his politics, worldviews, or agenda; I for one am proud to call Barack Obama my president, and was happy to see him elected (and reelected). This is not even about his competence in the Oval Office; for what it's worth, I find his intentions and ideas admirable, his character great, and his intelligence superb. Honestly, this isn't about Barack Obama; it's about everything else. It's about the machine that consumed him.

I was a senior in college in 2008. I was finishing a poly sci minor, taking at least three politic-heavy classes, and it seemed like everyone had something to say on the presidential election, in and out of the classroom. And when the results came in on election night? My god, what an atmosphere – a magnificent explosion of optimism I had never before seen in my life. The group I ran with wasn't even particularly pro-Obama, but even they couldn't help but be awestruck and a little tingly. The excitement was palpable. My roommate, girlfriend, and I shared a bottle of champagne in my apartment to ring in the momentous occasion, and two thirds of us didn't even vote for the guy. It just somehow seemed that things were gonna be alright.

And it wasn't just us, the college kids on college campuses. From what I could tell, the whole damn country – from housewives to businessmen to construction workers – was fired up to some degree. Even if we didn't believe in his political platform, we believed in what he stood for. We believed in hope, change, and positivity.

Over four years later, we still believe in those things,

but just slightly more than we believe in the Powerball or early retirement to a yacht in the Carribean. We believe because we want to, because we need to, and because no matter what happens, so many of us are idealists at our cores. But we don't believe it's in front of us, waiting to be snatched and cherished and drank up in all its delicious glory, like we did on November 4th, 2008. The bad guys, once again, have won. Nearly four years into the Obama presidency, there has been progress, but it's been slow at best and disheartening at worst. Again, I'm not putting this solely on the president – I have no idea how much, if any, is his fault. But the parties are more divided than ever, compromise is nonexistent, and pandering, partisanship, grandstanding, and lies reign supreme. The Grand Canyon lies in the aisle of congress, and the gap Obama promised to bridge has only grown wider. These people – these Republicans and Democrats – are not working for us. They are working for themselves. We are losing.

If Barack Obama couldn't change the conventional culture of Washington, with the way the country was lined up behind him after the inauguration, ready to go to Pluto and back, I'm fairly certain nobody can. The current culture cannot be changed; it needs to be blown up. So let's get out the dynamite, motherfuckers.

I don't think things are bad overall in our country. I would want to live nowhere else, and I love America as much as – if not more than – each and every Billy Ray with a confederate flag on the back of his truck. The truly wonderful part about the U.S. of A. is that living here still kicks ass no matter how screwed things are on Capitol Hill. At the time of this writing, the economy was still in the shitter, the national debt was growing by eighteen kazillion dollars every millisecond, we were still involved in too many foreign conflicts (each also costing a few kazillion each day), and party hacks on each side couldn't even eat a damn chicken sandwich without making it a divisive issue, and another way to show you that they're right and you're wrong. But all this, and I still wake up in a beautiful place every morning, have the opportunity to go to work in my chosen profession during the day, and cap things off with a delicious scotch or DQ Blizzard at night. How is that previous sentence NOT an embodiment of the American dream? Nobody starts out on a level playing field in life, but in this country, you can run or climb or dance as fast as - and in in whatever direction – you want. And I don't care how liberal, conservative, fascist, or anarchist you consider yourself – that's pretty damn cool.

This is the section where I'd rail against the way political polarization has driven a wedge between Americans. But there's not enough room here; that's another essay, or book, or collection of books. To summarize and spare you a lot of words, my thesis on the matter is this: the "picking sides" mentality mandated by the two-party system is counterproductive to rational discourse and progress, and it preys on basic, deeply ingrained human emotions. It is the exact opposite of what we should strive for, if we're at all interested in social progress. I'm not much into picking sides, and I have no honest idea who's "right" across the political spectrum. But I'm pretty sure that if you're either a die-hard Democrat or Republican, you're wrong.

In the end, I guess don't mean to tell you what to do with your vote in the upcoming election, or any election. All I ask is that you don't approach the polling booth with the intention of voting for who you see as the lesser of two evils. Not just in the presidential race, but all of them, because they are all vitally important. Spend some time researching the possibilities, and then decide what's really best for the country. Prepare with your head, and vote with your heart. Voting unconventionally isn't wasting your vote, but giving up and supporting the status quo is.

THE STAGES OF THE DOG

Dog Loving, Phase 1

I don't really get the dog thing. Most dog-lovers like to insinuate this makes me a bad person, but I disagree; I'm a bad person for entirely separate reasons. I've just never understood the connection some people make with dogs, or any pet for that matter. I have nothing against them – dogs are furry, often playful, and occasionally fun – but I just don't think they bring all that much to the table. They're just kind of there, waiting for you to take them out twice a day lest they shit on your carpet. People often talk of "companionship" they have with their animals. I'm not quite sure how something with which I cannot communicate could become my "companion," just as I don't know how I could form an emotional bond with a tree or the grill on my back porch. Hell, at least the grill produces delicious food; in the dog/human dynamic, *I'm* the one giving out the meals.

My girlfriend is one of these "dog people." She, of course, cannot fathom my indifference to the beasts. It seems I am a heartless monster. She cherishes the creature – Riley – and speaks in baby voices to it as it jumps and paws and knocks things over in anticipation of a treat or a walk or some other indulgence. The woman insists he is a beautiful animal – "Isn't he so CUTE?!?" she enthusiastically asks as she rubs the dog's belly. No, he isn't; he actually looks more like a mangy pound mutt that was born from a host of different breeds, taking one of the least desirable characteristics from each. Which is precisely what he is. But of course, I don't say this; instead I grit my teeth and nod my head. I lie to keep the peace.

What is it about having a pet that gets people so hot and bothered? Is it just comforting to constantly have another living creature near you? Are we really that lonely? "A man's best friend," the saying goes, but if your best friend is truly a slobbering critter that doesn't even know your name, I suggest you take up drinking.

The connection some people form with their dogs just seems a little extreme.

We can keep the dogs around; no need to euthanize them all or anything, as I've found over the years they do serve *some* purpose, if only one of distraction. I've been known to pet, play fetch with, and attempt to ride many a canine. But it's just never my canine – I have enough responsibilities in life that carving out the time to tie an animal to my hand and walk behind it twice a day has never seemed ideal. It appears I'm selfish. Or just rational. Either way, I'm in the minority.

I live in Colorado and spend a decent amount of time in downtown Denver, where dogs often seem to outnumber humans. Dogver, as I like to call it, is the definition of a "dog-friendly" city, with bountiful dog parks and grooming stations and cans in which to dump their shit. The city has a strong hippie streak, and for whatever reason hippies seem to gravitate to dogs (probably due in part to their similar hygiene) and hoard them by the bunches. It's not uncommon to see a head of dreadlocks out walking five separate beasts on five separate leashes.

This dog culture inevitably permeates the normal

people as well. The girlfriend is far from a hippie, but loves the dog as if she were one. She treats it like a family member, will certainly cry when the pooch dies – as she did for the last one – and considers it her first line of protection against strangers. All this despite the creature's major character flaws. The dog has a nasty temper that is hidden most of the time – in order to lull you into a false state of security – but will rear its ugly head at the most inopportune moments. Taking the dog for a leisurely stroll through the park, a friendly jogger will bend down to say hello, to which the beast responds spastically by trying to tear his or her nose off. In the middle of the night I will get up to piss, and upon returning to my side of the bed find the dog waiting for me. He stares me down in the darkness, then begins a low growl that turns into a fit of snarling and barks. All this for no apparent reason, from an animal that was sleeping peacefully just a minute ago. Thankfully, my man parts have steered clear of its wrath.

Dog Loving, Phase 2 (Two months later)

I suppose the dog isn't the worst thing in the world.

Somehow, in the face of the mounting evidence against it, my step-mutt has grown on me to a certain extent. I cannot explain this, and infer that it is a small part of the larger human logical leap that causes us to embrace these creatures in the first place. Regardless of its loose temper or refusal to be mounted and ridden like a miniature steed, the dog has redeeming characteristics. It seems to treat me like a pal, and I often can't help but reciprocate. After all, what human friend would voluntarily lick my feet in the name of sanitation?

Perhaps there is some use for these animals after all. I will not be rushing to the breeder requesting a puppy of my own anytime soon, but I can tolerate and sporadically enjoy a canine. Just as long as I am not responsible for it, and it is well-behaved in public. As long as you don't spend more money on dog food than you do your own, I will still not understand your dog affliction but will make an effort to accept it. I still think you're weird, but clean its shit up and we're cool.

Dog Loving, Phase 3 (Six months later)
Riley greets me enthusiastically when I come home. I like that.

He barks and jumps in circles, rejoicing in my return. He's so adorable in his bandana, I can't help but laugh and pet the shit out of him. I'm going to take him on a nice long walk...

Wait, what's going on? What am I turning in to? This is an animal that just a few months ago I wanted euthanized. Surely he didn't change his tune so quickly. Am I blind? Am I being brainwashed? WHAT IS HAPPENING TO ME?!?

Dog Loving, Phase 4 (One Year later)
O. M. G. Riley is the CUTEST when he jumps up on the bed and hangs out with me. I rub his stomach and scratch his belly. It's just so nice to have a friendly dog like him around.

I don't really understand why some people think he's mean; he'll only growl or bark if he doesn't like you. And if that's the case, you've clearly done something wrong. Yes, he almost bit my coworker's wife's face off the other day, but it was hardly a big deal. For some reason, they left my house shortly after – weirdoes. It wouldn't kill them to get to know the little guy. I've always said he's delightful.

And that's how they get us – it's a slow simmer that turns our indifference into love, and it happens so subtly that we don't even notice until we're voluntarily speaking to the pooch in some sort of canine gibberish. This is where we learn we have no real control over them; the dogs are in charge. It's all a damn racket if you ask me, and I'm not exactly sure what this means for the human race.

QUITTING COLD STONE (AND OTHER STRUGGLES)

Now if you'll kindly excuse me, I need to be taking Riley out.

THE BEST DEFENSE AGAINST ASSHOLES

The other day, I was confronted with the strong urge to punch someone in the face. This person was being a dick – as dicks are wont to do – and certainly seemed to deserve it. If you know me personally, you know that there was no chance I'd *actually* just punch someone in the face, and in the end I gathered myself and walked away. Number one; it was the right thing to do, and number two; I'm not a face-puncher. I wouldn't win many fights. But the issue here isn't about *actually* punching someone in the face for being an asshole; it's about *wanting* to do it. And this is an urge most of us experience from time to time.

No matter who you are, where you live, or what type of personality you have, chances are you have enemies. Whether this is your doing or not, it just seems to happen; at some point in one's life, a relationship (or sometimes many relationships) will form from mutual dislike. We're going to assume it's more their fault than yours, if only because that's what it always feels like. And this is fine; blame them. I do. They are, after all, the asshole.

QUITTING COLD STONE (AND OTHER STRUGGLES)

The important question here is how to deal with these situations. You certainly *can* go the face-punching route, but honestly that won't do much for you long term. You may get momentary satisfaction, but instead of everyone lifting you over their heads and cheering like they do in movies (and probably your imagination), they'll probably just back away slowly or ask what the hell is wrong with you. Another option is to give the jerkoff a proverbial "piece of your mind," which can feel outstanding, but public reaction to this is – again – usually lukewarm at best. Something about making a scene.

Physical or verbal violence are never the best option, and as I walked away from the situation in question, I reminded myself of something. No matter what the circumstance, the single best way to deal with nasty people in your life:

Do well.

That's it. Just do well in whatever you do. You don't even have to see, talk to, or think about the assholes at large. All you need to do is do your thing, and do it the best you can. Accomplish, achieve, explore, discover, succeed. Win. Decide what you want to do, then go do it. Put in time. Wake up an hour earlier, drink another cup of coffee, and give yourself the extra edge you need to make the world your bitch. Try something new, try harder at something you already do, or try to do less of something that's detrimental to you. Turn off the TV, get off your ass, and *do*. Read, create, and be curious. Stop worrying about failing and instead actually fail. Then learn, try again, and succeed. After that, succeed more. Unhook the plow, unchain the shackles, and *let the beast out*.

These things are the best way to get back at the people that don't like you, because seeing you succeed *kills* those people. They hate it. Your happiness, positive energy, and overall prosperity carry more weight than any number of punches in the face or roundhouse kicks. Use it. Chase your bliss and find your inner ninja while those other bastards watch from the sidelines. Ignore them and succeed, and their blood will boil. This isn't about rubbing it in either; you don't need to. You don't need to deal with them in any way, because they're insignificant. They don't count. And anyway, they'll know.

What counts is that you identify what you want in life, and then wake up every damn day and bust your ass in pursuit of that goal. Rise, flourish, and hone your craft. Thrive. Hell, go for a vacation. Take a drive. Find something new. Expand your mind and grow as a human being. The rest will follow.

These things take time, and the gratification is exponentially more delayed than a snap reaction to a nasty person. But I'll be damned if it isn't exponentially more satisfying.

Why should you trust my advice? Honestly, I can't say. You have no reason to. I haven't lived that long, haven't had many exponential successes, and haven't even punched anyone in the face (and thus wouldn't truly know the feeling). But don't take my word for it – try it. Put away the retaliation and the snarky responses and the stooping to *their* level for a minute, and take the high road. Stop worrying about how you'll respond to asshole comments, or what you'll say to make him or her feel as bad as they make you feel. Live your life, find your happiness and succeed at what you do. Kick today's ass. And if you don't find it a billion times more satisfying, then try a different approach. But I bet you won't need to.

Just do well.

ALL OVERRATED LIST, PART 2

Now, back to the bashing!

Jack Kerouac
I admit I'm basing my opinion of him purely on one book, but that book is widely regarded as his definitive work. I avoided reading On the Road for quite some time despite prodding from my more well-read friends, but eventually caved and gave it a shot. Years later, I'm still waiting for the supposed brilliance to sink in.

The book, as far as I can tell, is a rambling stream of consciousness about a guy bumming across the U.S. It doesn't have much real structure or flow, and most of the scenes consist of a hyper drunk named Dean Moriarty screaming "YES!" while watching some jazz band or shouting "I dig you man!" at strangers. This – like most things in the book – is probably supposed to represent something grandiose and important, but to me just represents uninspired storylines and an uninteresting character. On the Road is said to be the voice of the "Beat" generation, and it very well might be – if that generation was boring and poorly written.

The book is more or less based on Kerouac's life in the 1940's. While it is largely autobiographical, most of the names were changed and I assume at least some of the passages were works of fiction. Maybe they all should've been, because as a true story the book kind of blows. Basically, I can sum up the majority of it as follows: Sal (the protagonist) and his friends have no money. Despite this, they avoid work at all costs. They get drunk (and probably do some drugs) and hang out and talk about how life is, like, such a trip man. Then they talk about how poor they are. Everything they have is shitty, they're hungry, the car barely starts and the roof leaks. They bum somewhere for a while, then move on and bum somewhere else for a while. They listen to jazz and Dean yells about how cool it is. Dean pisses some lady off. They pack and move again. They're still poor as shit and see no real reason to get a job.

That's pretty much it. All this through fairly pedestrian writing; every passage is told so dryly and literally, it feels like Kerouac is reciting the nuances of metamorphic rock formation rather than telling a story. An American classic, ladies and gentlemen!

Dave Matthews Band

Talented as hell – I will concede you this. But I cannot figure out why anyone would willingly buy/spend the time illegally downloading their music, much less stampede to their concerts and festivals in droves like they do. Is it the weed thing? Matthews and his cronies are open potheads, and somewhere along the line they got labeled a "stoner band," so naturally every dreadlocked college dropout in the country is like, way into their music. I've never understood this thinking though; if you're going to follow a band because of their use of the marijuana, you have a lot of rock bands to follow. Like most of them. Maybe you need to be high to understand the system.

Anyway, through the intentional listening of at least three full DMB albums in an effort to figure out what the fuck it's all about, I still can't crack the code. All I hear is rhythmic mumbling and occasional horse sounds into the microphone. Seriously, the guy doesn't even sing; it just sounds like he continually contorts his lips and blows, kind of like a human didgeridoo. The music itself, however, is actually quite impressive. That's not that I think it's good, just as a jumbled collection of premiere auto parts don't make a good car; the individual musicians and instrumentations are dripping with talent and imagination, but they aren't assembled in a meaningful carriage. So I think the music is great...it's just that the songs suck. It's the equivalent of Steve Vai, Yngwie Malmsteen, or the 2011 Philadelphia Eagles; a lot of good there, but nobody was able to mold the individual parts into a cohesive and meaningful whole. It's just a lot of raggedy freelancing, which can be fun at times, but won't win the Super Bowl (or even make the playoffs).

And what's with the whole "jam band" thing? Just because Dave chooses to strum the same chords over and over for 20 minutes straight, doesn't make it "jamming." It's a damn disgrace to compare them to bands like the Allman Brothers and Gov't Mule, whose inspired solos and improvisations tear the metaphorical roof off late into the night. Those are jams. Dave Matthews just plays really long songs.

At least that's what I think. There's a good possibility I'm just missing "it." I am, after all, not high.

Joking About How the Weatherman is Usually Wrong

You know the drill. You're in an unfamiliar or awkward situation, the conversation turns stagnant, and someone falls back on the old standby, the small talk of all small talk: the weather.

"Would be nice if was a little warmer, eh?"

"Oh yeah. Sure. Would be nice. Still beats snow though."

"Definitely, definitely. Beats snow."

(Pause)

"It's supposed to get nicer this weekend though, isn't it?"

"It is! Yeah, they said it should be up in the 70's by Saturday. You never know though – they're usually wrong."

This is one big lie that is constantly perpetuated across our small-talking American culture: the weatherman is usually wrong. I'm not sure if it was grandfathered in from a time when people predicted the elements by licking their fingers and sticking them in the air, and we just haven't been able to shake it. But this is just flat out untruthful; the weatherman isn't usually wrong. In fact, he's barely ever wrong – I'd venture a guess of around 92 percent accuracy. I'm not a meteorologist, nor am I a member of any weatherman unions or lobby groups. I'm just a guy that calls them like I see them. Seriously, watch the news tonight. The exchange between anchor and weather person will probably go something like this:

Anchor: "...and that's what happened last night on 'Dancing with the Stars.' Now it's time to go over to Paul in the SUPER Doppler Storm-Tracking Weather Center, 6.0. Paul, can we expect some sun this week?"

Weather guy: "We sure can, Tom! In fact, a lot of sun, because it's going to be HOT the next few days."

And you know what'll happen? It'll probably be hot the next few days. If he forecasts rain, it'll probably rain. Sure, maybe it will be only .3 inches instead of the half inch he predicted, but who cares? It fucking rained. That's what he said would happen. He was right. Accept it.

Fireworks

And parades, for that matter. These are things we got excited about as six year-olds and for some reason are still expected to regard with the same enthusiasm. And strangely, most of us do. To be clear, I'm not talking about the do-it-yourself fireworks, where you light a fuse, throw it/run for cover, and try not to blow your fingers off. Those are awesome. I'm talking about communal fireworks; essentially watching others carry out the above events, just from a few miles away.

Every July 4th in America (and some other days too, depending on where you live), we go to "watch the fireworks." We pile in cars, show up to an overcrowded location, spend 30 minutes looking for parking, try to avoid snot-nosed kids spilling their ice cream cones on your shoes, and cram into a sweaty and loud park or parking lot, always getting an undesirable viewing location because the good ones were taken by people that showed up three hours ago. We then wait until sunset – the universal fireworks start time –and then wait 30 minutes longer because nothing ever starts on time.

When they finally start shooting them off, we sit back and ooh and aww at colorful explosions in the sky for 20 minutes or so, generally culminating in a "grand finale" of more fireworks, just shot off faster. Admittedly, the first few times you see this, it's damn impressive. The sights and sounds of colorful airborne bombs blowing up in the night sky is quite the experience for a firework virgin. But then we see them again. And again. And 300 more times throughout our lives. It really gets mundane at this point; there are slight variations in fireworks shows, but they're all pretty much the same. Really, there haven't been many technological advances made – if they could create the image of moving rocket ships or a guy with a sword fighting a dragon, that would be exciting and totally worth the hassle. But alas, it's pretty much always just a green or blue or red explosion. And the hassle still exists, with the crowds and the parking and the snot-nosed kids. Not my idea of a good time. Also, get off my lawn.

ALL UNDERRATED LIST, PART 2

Pure Maple Syrup
I realize most educated eaters (and people of Vermont) recognize the inherent and life-altering goodness of maple syrup. But it still seems to get overlooked on a consistent basis; maybe because it's all the way on the top shelf at the grocery store, or because it costs three or four times as much as its processed Aunt Jemima counterpart. It's a delicacy of sorts, and I get that. But my god it's delicious.

The issue here is what we call "upgrade over alternative." For most foods, if you pay the few extra bucks to get the "high quality" version, it'll improve your meal incrementally. For example, if you go for the extra choice Boar's Head deli meat instead of whatever slimy concoction comes in those plastic Oscar Meyer packages, you'll have a damn good sandwich, but a sandwich nonetheless. It's an improvement for sure, but nothing life-changing. The same goes for high-quality milk, bacon, and ground beef. But the jump from the standard supermarket "syrup" to some authentic, pure Vermont maple? Much, much more

– it's practically exponential. Real maple syrup can turn a drab frozen waffle breakfast into a borderline religious experience. It's like a damn explosion of peace, harmony, and everlasting life in your mouth. I'm convinced the path to Zion is lined with large maple trees, all dripping this divine concoction as we skip along on our way to eternal salvation. It's that good. If I were a member of Congress, I'd introduce legislation that would require breakfast joints to ditch the cheap stuff in favor of the genuine article. If we can regulate the quality of gasoline and medications, then why not syrup? It's a matter of national interest.

Free Refills

In many regions, we've come to expect free refills on fountain beverages at restaurants, so we tend to overlook it. But it should really be a high point in one's day – just think about how awesome it is for someone to give you another one of something you bought, absolutely free of charge, as many times in a row as you want. What if this happened with burgers or t-shirts or dental procedures? It would be considered amazing. Yet we've been spoiled by the free refill, and thus don't give it the credit it deserves.

I've heard that in some corners of the U.S. – I'm looking at you, Northeast – free refills are not the norm. This is not okay. Growing up in the Midwest, I became accustomed to them at an early age, and can't fathom life without a complimentary Coke after I guzzle down my first Coke. Not offering this is borderline un-American – I'm fairly sure the Constitution mentions free refills on fountain soda somewhere. If you refuse to provide this, the terrorists win.

Awkwardness

Seriously. We as a society have run from awkwardness for so long, fearing it like a fire-breathing, sword-wielding dragon of social blunder. An awkward situation surely is on our national (and global) "Top Five Things to Avoid at all Costs" list, alongside gunfights, cancer, public speaking, and civil political discourse. The mere thought of standing, hands in pockets, in a social circle of moderately unfamiliar people, everyone drawing a blank on what to say next...it's terrifying. Our skin crawls at the notion of unbroken silence between strangers, or inappropriate questions asked aloud, or a strange stumble in front of a group. Improper social grace is abhorred.

I say no more. Rather than fleeing the scene of the alleged crime, I say we embrace the awkward, and thus marginalize the power it holds over us. The truth is, there's nothing wrong with finding oneself in a clumsy, unpolished situation from time to time, even if it's a result of one's own doing. Why must we be comfortable all the time? Can't we accidentally – or even willfully – step into occasional discomfort, then just kind of stay there for a while, looking around, chuckling to ourselves, and taking it all in? Hell, we might learn something. I'm not sure what, but surely most lessons are found outside the comfort zone, no? And surely a man of greatest self-actualization is one that can remain cool, calm, and debonair in the face of extreme awkwardness. Let's stop running from the stuff, and instead boldly and oafishly stumble straight in the middle of it, with our arms swinging wildly and a half-deranged look on our collective face. Let's embrace the awkward.

Biloxi, Mississippi

The most underrated vacation destination in the United States, bar none. To be fair, its rating is so nonexistent that even if the Biloxi experience involved nothing more than chowing down the sloppy grits and limp bacon at the local Waffle Houses, it would be underrated. But it's so much more than that.

Now, it *does* involve the Waffle House thing, but other stuff too. I went to Biloxi on a family vacation in high school. It was spring break, and many of my contemporaries were fleeing to Mexico or Daytona Beach or somewhere equally as sunny and cliché. They of course were baffled by my destination. *Really, Sam? Mississippi?*

I admit it seemed suspect. Who voluntarily goes to Mississippi? I certainly hadn't until then, and had never considered it until my parents announced that was where we were headed. And I guess I didn't question it – probably because my folks had an excellent track record with vacations (the aforementioned Branson debacle notwithstanding) – until those around me started to.

Each time I told a friend or coworker where I was going during the week off, they responded with a blank stare, followed by a simple question of, "What's there?" And truth be told, I really had no idea, but I nonetheless stammered something about golf and a beach and a whole lot of casinos. It's what the brochures said, and it was all pretty unconvincing. By the time we left, I'd succumbed to public perception enough to believe the trip was going to suck. *Mississippi? What is there to do there? Why aren't we going to Mazatlan? What are these parents thinking?* I hated the vacation before it started.

And when we arrived, I didn't see much to immediately change my mind. The world outside the plane window was rainy, grey, and all-around uninspiring. Our baggage was delayed. The airport was full of fat people, all seemingly bitching at one another as they waddled along. The forecast called for rain all week. I did not like this place. Of course, being the little bastard I was, I made sure my parents were aware I was dissatisfied with the trip, and would not be enjoying my time. It's a wonder they didn't push me out of the rental car. I went to bed that night with a frown on my face and a whine in my heart.

In the morning, I woke up and grumbled, then walked to the sliding glass door. I opened the blinds and stepped out on the hotel balcony, and everything changed; gone was the drab and boring landscape, replaced with the sun-soaked beauty of a delightful gulf town. The hotel looked out over the beach – well-maintained and not at all crowded – and palm trees stretched across the horizon. The shore was lined with casinos, but not the loud and obnoxious variety found in Vegas; they were friendly, understated slices of southern hospitality. *This might actually work* I thought to myself. I turned on the TV, and suddenly the forecast called for sun and highs in the upper 70's all week. My father and I drove to the golf course, where we split a sixer and played a stress-free nine. We returned to find my mom and brother playing Frisbee on a nearly empty, almost sparkling beach, and proceeded as such for most of the afternoon. That evening, we had a delightful seafood dinner as my parents slipped me an occasional cocktail – none of the wait staff seemed to mind.

The rest of the week pretty much played out like that. The locals were accommodating and happy to have us, the water was warm, and the food and beverage were very reasonably priced. I got my first taste of Waffle House, and while I found I don't care for grits, it was fun to try something foreign (which, coming from north central Minnesota, it was). It seemed nobody owned a watch, and life moved accordingly. I cannot remember a more relaxing week in my life, and came away from it with a new respect for the south – or at least Biloxi, Mississippi. If you ever find yourself short on funds but long on time, do yourself a favor and give it a try. I'll take it over the bump and grind of a Virginia Beach spring break any week of the year.

CUSTOMER SERVICE BY COMCAST

Not too long ago, I heard a rumor that the reason the Comcast cable company started calling its services "Xfinity" was because they had such an atrocious reputation for customer service, that the only way they could get back in the public's good graces was by rebranding and making us think they were someone else. I never looked into the claim, but after a recent episode with the company's fabled customer service department, I can pretty much consider it gospel.

My roommate Brendon moved out. After living together for two years, he got a job in Berkeley, California, and hit the high road. I'm happy for him, as the position he took was a professional upgrade and he moved to a truly beautiful place. But this roommate shift affected me negatively in two ways: one, it removed seemingly continuous access to the best wings on the planet. Brendon liked to eat, *loved* to eat wings, and somewhere along the line realized that to get the perfect blend of sweetness and spice, he'd have to take matters into his own hands. So he did;

the man bought his own deep fryer, and worked tirelessly on perfecting his recipe, resulting in what was easily the finest wing sauce I have ever tasted. It's a spicy buffalo of sorts, with just the right amount of heat and a tangy zip that keeps you perpetually reaching for one more. Seriously, if Elvis were still alive, he would've said to hell with the peanut butter, banana, and bacon sandwiches and flown to our house for wings instead. They're that good.

Anyway, the other problem was that I had to put all the bills at the house in my name. Brendon took care of it when he lived there, so his move made it necessary for me to take control of trash, electric, water, and cable. This is normally nothing more than a minor nuisance, and for most of the utilities that's all it was. But then it came time to set up a new cable account with Comcast, and I began hemorrhaging hours of my life attempting to get the service up and running, without making much progress.

It began with an internet setup. I'd researched and found the package I wanted, and attempted to use Xfinity's online signup process to buy it. I only wanted cable television and internet, because that's all anyone wants, despite the fact that Comcast inexplicably tries to shove home phone bundles down everyone's collective throat. (Seriously, home phone? Could I get a fax machine and pager with that too?). But after enough scouring, I did find a "double play" bundle that would suit my needs just fine. I followed the prompts for the setup, but when it came time to select an installation window, there was no option to self-install. I knew this is a possibility, because my friends had told me they'd done it that way, and being the cheap ass I am, I wasn't about to pay someone to come to my house and perform a simple service of which I'm perfectly capable. Plus, you have to schedule one of those weird time windows, and end up sitting at your home from noon to four on a Wednesday afternoon waiting for the technician to arrive. These are the hours you never get back.

So I called. My request seemed simple enough:

"Hi, I want this specific package shown on your website, but I'd like to install it myself."

His response was equally simple, but not very helpful:

"Yes, hello. I can allow you to install the equipment yourself, but can't give you that specific deal over the phone. That one is an 'online-only' special."

Me: "Very well, I'll go back and sign up for it online. But surely it's possible to select self-install in the online signup process. Am I just missing it?"

Him: "Yes, it should be possible."

Me: "Okay. Where is it?"

Him: "I'm not exactly sure. But I think it's on there somewhere."

Me: "Any general ideas?"

Him: "No. Now go forth and waste the rest of your day searching for some possibly-existent setup option on our intentionally confusing website." (I'm paraphrasing here.)

So I did. And guess what? Never found it.

Instead, I just figured I'd go ahead and complete the process online and select a random install time. Then I'd call them and let them know they didn't need to dispatch the setup team, because I'd pick up the gear and install it myself.

It was all going fine until the *very* end of the online process, when I was informed that to complete my setup, I'd need to enter an online support chat with a Comcast rep, just to make sure everything was in order. It was standard procedure, they told me. Annoying, yes, but I figured it would just be a few more minutes of questions of confirmation, and then I'd be out of there.

I was connected with Lloyd, who spent the first 10 minutes of the chat – already much longer than I'd hoped – rehashing all the service preferences I'd already entered earlier in the process. It was almost as if I had to sign up for everything again, only in AOL Instant Messenger form. Why would I have to repeat information that should already be in their system? Maybe Lloyd was just lonely and none of his friends were online to Google Chat with him. Whatever the reason, it was getting on my nerves.

Then the son of a bitch tried to upsell me.

ACTUAL XFINITY ONLINE CHAT MESSAGES:
(Please disregard any grammatical errors in Lloyd's text. I do believe he was still learning.)

Lloyd: By the way, Sam, we are now offering a new low cost Service Protection Plan that will provide you with worry-free protection for any potential in-home wiring problem with your cable TV, high speed internet or telephone service. With the protection plan, if anything goes wrong with the inside wiring a professional trained technician will identify the problem and fix it quickly. This plan will provide you with an alternative to potential service call charges, which can be costly. This low cost service protection plan is only $3.99 a month and is added to your monthly bill for your convenience. Would you like to have the Service Protection Plan added to your account today?

Sam: no

Terse, yes, but I was tired of the process and in no mood to be solicited. Lloyd was initially understanding but ultimately unabated.

Lloyd: Not a problem. In any case, you may want to ask our technician during install about our Service Protection Plan. They will explain to you in further details the benefits of that plan and if you like to have it added to your services, they can do that for you as well.

Lloyd: Sam, here is a great news for you! You are qualified to sign up for our new Starter Xfinity Triple Play Bundle: cable, internet, and phone in 1 package for

$99.00/month for the entire year.

Lloyd: With this package you will get to enjoy over 80 digital cable channels plus thousands of ON DEMAND movies and shows, 12 to 15 mbps internet speed with POWERBOOST and UNLIMITED nationwide calling phone service with 12 popular calling features for FREE. This would be the perfect time to sign up for the bundle at a discounted rate.

Lloyd: Isn't it wonderful to have all 3 services in 1 bill at 1 low price?

Sam: Can you please just give me the package I signed up for? That would be good customer service. Thanks.

Lloyd: Sure, no problem.

Lloyd: It is without contract, right?

Sam: Scroll up please.

I wasn't providing him any more information that I'd already entered. He could go dig it up if he had to. I was in full blown disgruntled customer mode at this point, and I wasn't even technically a customer yet. And nobody was forcing me to go with Comcast...but they're pretty much the only dual cable/internet provider in the area. So I kind of needed them. *Sigh.* I kept with the chat. Lloyd kept inaccurately recounting my information.

Lloyd: And it is Double Play Digital Preferred and High Speed Internet $89.99 a month for 6 months.

Lloyd: I just want to confirm it.

Sam: 84.99

Lloyd: Yes I am sorry. It is $84.99 a month for 6 months.

Lloyd: And after 6 months, it is $104.99 a month.

Lloyd: Thank you so much.
Lloyd: I am still processing your order
Lloyd: Please give me 2 to 3 minutes.

Oh sure, Lloyd, take as much time as you need. Really, I don't have anything else to do. I enjoy sitting in online chat rooms with people I don't know asking me to repeat information when I just want to PURCHASE CABLE TV AND INTERNET FROM YOUR COMPANY.

Then, I decided to take control. He clearly wouldn't know which installation option I'd chosen, so I decided to tell him that I'd selected self-install. This would probably make his head explode in confusion, but at least then the chat would be over.

Lloyd: By the way, you can get our discounted one time installation fee of $34.99. We'll give you a recap of your order once I am done processing.

Lloyd: Please provide me the nearest cross intersection to your home so the installer would be easier to find your new location and the appropriate number that we can contact you. Thank you.

Sam: I selected the self install option. Can you not see the info I entered?

Lloyd: I understand that. In the order, there's one time installation fee of $20 and there is a shipment fee of $20.00.

Sam: Well I'm installing it, so there shouldn't be an installation fee. And I can pick it up at the Boulder Comcast location, so don't worry about shipping it.

Lloyd: It is possible to pick it up the Self Installation Kit however, you must go directly to Comcast service center.

QUITTING COLD STONE (AND OTHER STRUGGLES)

Oh really, the Comcast service center? Hmm. I was expecting to meet someone in the parking lot behind a Taco Bell and move the gear from his rusted GMC Jimmy to my car. But if you want to do it another way, I suppose we could.

At least I'd gotten the self-install thing figured out. Lloyd rambled on for a few more minutes, asking more questions that probably had nothing to do with cable service at this point.

Lloyd: "So you prefer Dove soap, is that correct?"
Me: "No, I'm an Irish Spring man. You should know this already."
Lloyd: "Oh yes, of course. I am just making sure."

Eventually I just asked to be excused from the chat, and Lloyd granted my wish. I honestly didn't know if my service was set up or not. When the chat window closed, there was one of those "Did we answer all your questions and help you out real good? Click here to take a short 30-question survey!" links. I clicked the link so as to give them a piece of my mind, and got an "internal server error" message.

Of course.

To try to sort things out and confirm my setup, I called Comcast. After a lengthy hold, I got an operator and explained the situation. Basically, I said, I just want to know if I'm good to go. The woman informed me she couldn't check the system for my records (because that makes sense), but if I got as far as the online chat session, my account was "almost certainly" set up.

So I went to the Comcast service center to pick up my gear. After waiting in a short line (20 minutes tops) I was summoned to the help counter by a college-aged woman with a nose ring. I gave her my info and she typed away for a few seconds before informing me, "Oh, it looks like they didn't actually set you up."

Mother of shit. All of that for nothing? My fruitless phone calls? My hours spent online? My redundant conversation with Lloyd? AND I HAD NOTHING TO SHOW FOR IT? The question now was not *if* I would kick a puppy when I left, but how many I could kick before the day was done.

"No problem though," she said. "I can get you the same deal. Actually, I can do better." Her voice was monotone as she pecked away at that keyboard, but my eyes lit up. "Let's make it $79.99 a month, and lock that price in for a year instead of six months. Were you planning on getting a DVR?"

"Yes," I replied. That cost $16.99 a month, but was totally worth it.

"Cool, I'll throw one in for free. And I'll give you free HBO for a year. Sound good?"

Good? How about "you're the most beautiful of all of God's creations, the most perfect thing I've ever laid eyes on. I weep at your kindness and marvel at your generosity"? I was dumbfounded; I can't remember the girl's name – probably Destani or Misti or something else ending in an "i" – but she had singlehandedly wiped out a full day's worth of Comcast's incompetence and frustration with a few keystrokes and an ounce of compassion. I considered making love to her right then and there, but then realized that wasn't an appropriate response and I'd probably be arrested, free DVR or not. Either way, I couldn't believe it.

"Um, thank you..." was all I could manage as my mouth gaped in awe. She finished the setup, had me sign a few things, and within five minutes I was on my way, gear in hand.

Comcast execs, Lloyd, and every deadbeat I talked to on the phone: you could all learn something from Destani or Misti or something else ending in an "i." I have no explanation for her random act of customer service, and clearly it isn't in line with your corporate code, but she is a shining light in an industry of darkness and hold music. I suggest you promote her to CEO immediately and live by her creed. At least it would save you the cost of rebranding again in the future.

SOME THOUGHTS ON THE ELECTION

(Written the day after Election Day 2012, when Barack Obama was reelected for a second term as President of the United States. For some reason, it seemed like an especially long election season, as the attack ads and nasty sound bites ran on TV almost constantly in the final few months (especially in the swing state of Colorado, where I live). The political process has always made me simultaneously frustrated and fascinated, and this is sort of a manifestation of both of those things. It's more of a commentary on the discourse surrounding the election than the election itself, and in a way is an extension of the "Wasting Your Vote" essay.)

- I did not vote for Barack Obama, but I will stand behind and support him as my president. I will champion compromise in congress and wherever else it can make meaningful progress. I will not pretend the president is evil (for he is not), and I will not intentionally roadblock his policies just because he has a certain letter by his name. Grow the fuck up.

QUITTING COLD STONE (AND OTHER STRUGGLES)

- The state of political discourse in America is basically two grown men hurling insults at each other from across the country. Think about that.

- Please stop pretending that everyone that doesn't agree with you is an idiot. They're just forming opinions based on what they've seen in their lives.

- At some point, accountability needs to become important for our elected officials. We're sick of being lied to, but it continues to happen because we willingly accept it without repercussions, time and time again. Take a look at the promises the candidates made before election, compare it to what actually happened, and vote accordingly. It's rarely just one person's fault, but if they're going to promise it, they'd better damn well be able to deliver.

- For the love of god, stop pretending there are only two candidates. I've already gone on about this elsewhere.

- It's a tremendous blessing that we have so many people in this country that actually give a shit. If you did your research and then casted an informed ballot, you should be proud of yourself.

- We need to be done jumping aboard the sound bite bandwagon during campaigns. That goes for "binders full of woman," "47%," "the private sector's doing fine," and plenty of others I'm glad I don't remember. We're all aware of how far they're taken out of context, and that they don't mean what we pretend they mean. Perpetuating sound bites makes us part of the problem. And using them in jokes is boring and unfunny.

- As Sir Winston Churchill once said, "You have enemies? Good. That means you've stood for something, sometime in your life." Continue to fight for what you believe in, but do so civilly, and entertain other viewpoints at least occasionally. Turning on Rachel Maddow (if you're a Democrat) or Rush Limbaugh (if you're a Republican) does not count.

- Continue to not give a shit what celebrities think.

I love you all, and God bless America.

Sam

(P.S. I wrote that first paragraph the morning of Election Day. Just left the name blank.)

WHAT IS THE DEAL WITH AIRLINE TRAVEL?

Sometimes as I stand on the far side of the security x-ray machine barefoot, holding my belt-less pants up with my hands and waiting for my carry-on items to emerge on the other side, I ponder the intricacies of airline travel. It's a humorous departure from everyday social norms – all these strangers packed together, removing their shoes and belts and putting them back on in unison, then proceeding to their respective gates where they'll sit together in one giant room, trying to leave at least one seat between them and the nearest stranger. Where else in life do we get such a large and diverse group of people together just to have them try to avoid each other at all costs?

Airline travel is at once fascinating and annoying, but for most veteran travelers it's far more of the latter. Consider, for example:

Checking Bags
This used to be a normal part of going to the airport, but now we avoid it like awkward conversation with that

lady from your wife's office. Why? They're charging us now. The ol' recession of 2007 and some combination of regulation and deregulation have had the airlines hurting financially for some time now, so this is their master plan for a revenue boost. At least $20 per bag, sometimes more, depending on the airline (unless you fly Southwest, in which case bags are free, but it's also the airline equivalent of traveling by city bus...so is it really worth it?).

So do we grin, bear it, and pay the money? Hell no! Anytime you try to get the general public to pay for something it had previously gotten for free, the people will react as if you're attempting to eat their children. Instead of ponying up the extra cash, we now stretch our carry-on allotment to the max; staying up late at night studying the carry-on rules, busting out the measuring tape to make sure we get the maximum inch allotments on our bags, and stuffing those things full until the zippers burst. We cram a checked-bag's worth of stuff into one carry-on and one personal item. I consider it a personal victory every time I can avoid checking a bag, and judging by the inordinate number of roller bags packing the overhead bins on every plane, I'm not alone.

The Security Line

The aforementioned removal of shoes and belts is the climax, but before that we're required to stand in a switch-backing, theme-park style rope line for 30 minutes or so. Eventually we reach a seated and apparently hungover TSA agent, who gives our boarding pass and ID a quick once over and waves us past. This agent is wearing latex gloves, which is somewhat concerning; the gloves seem to indicate that there is enough sickness and germs in the building to make hand protection necessary. In which case, I start to wonder what else they aren't telling us, and why am *I* not wearing gloves, but then I'm quickly ushered along.

We reach the conveyor belt for the x-ray machine, where businessmen, wives, uncles, and families of 17 are

QUITTING COLD STONE (AND OTHER STRUGGLES)

frantically stripping down and throwing their shit in plastic bins. This part actually makes me happy, because it's the one time in the terminal everyone actually acts like they're trying to get somewhere instead of just sauntering through the building and casually gazing up at the wonders of airport architecture. It's a frenzied effort to not disappoint the person behind us, which taking too long to clear our pockets of loose change and gum wrappers would certainly do. We remove our laptops from our carry-on bags and isolate them in separate bins, while waiting to be called up to the x-ray machine or recently minted body-scanner.

Throughout the first 18 years of my life, the airport x-ray machine was my sworn enemy. Over the course of countless flights in that time frame, I don't believe I once successfully made it through on the first try. *BEEEP* the machine would scream in dissatisfaction, requiring me to go back to the front of the line and think about what I'd done. No matter what I removed from my body – wallet, keys, belt, pants – I couldn't seem to pass the airport's advanced threat detection technology, and usually ended up having to be wanded. This is of course the part where the (always male) TSA agent pulls you aside and requires you to spread your legs while he gropes your privates with a metal-detecting safety wand, which makes perfect sense to do to a clueless 12-year-old white kid with Kool-Aid stains around his mouth. I'm sure I looked like a terrorist.

For whatever reason, in my adult life I've suddenly been able to avoid the beeps for the most part and actually pass security on the first try. Not sure why – maybe the technology became more efficient, or maybe I stopped carrying bombs on my person. Nowadays, they usually choose to pull me into the body scanner – that newfangled machine that makes you stand spread eagle and takes a photo that shows your naked body or whatever – instead of the standard metal detector. I assume this is because they're just interested in seeing me nude. So I take it as a compliment.

In any event, we eventually emerge on the other side and struggle to maintain our balance while we put our shoes back on and re-thread our belts through the belt loops. It's odd, for strangers to be removing and putting their belts back on together in a public place at such a high rate, without a second thought of its oddity. I might start doing this at the grocery store and see if anyone joins in.

Escalators and Moving Walkways

In order to reach our terminal, we're generally required to walk 7-10 miles through other parts of the airport. And during this pilgrimage, travelers are almost certain to come upon an escalator or moving walkway, which are both universally used wrong. The purpose of these marvels of technology is to move humanity *faster* through highly condensed areas, and thus increasing efficiency of travel. Contrary to popular belief, it is NOT to provide people (especially Americans) with one more excuse *not* to move, and to avoid what little exercise one gets from walking or climbing a flight of stairs. Alas, the latter purpose is generally how they're used, but this is okay; I understand you may have had a long day of work or travel, and maybe you just want to rest up a little bit by dropping your bags and ceasing movement for the duration of the ride. This is not a big deal – we all need a break from time to time – and I'm in no position to tell you how to live. But could you at least get the hell out of my way? Most escalators and moving walkways have ample room to fit two grown adults side by side, probably due to those of us that like to use them as our own personal lazy train. The idea is that if you simply *must* phone it in, those of us that don't live your hard and draining life can continue moving past you. This does not work, however, when you stop dead in the middle of the track with three oversized suitcases and a handful of children at your side. This actually completely ruins it for everyone behind you that is not a lazy ass.

So, in summary: when faced with these situations,

either **a)** walk, or **b)** move aside, so the rest of us can.

The Gate
After we brave human traffic jams and mass belt removals, we're rewarded with the gate – our final destination before the actual airplane. Upon showing up at the gate, the cluster of seats for travelers to sit in while waiting to board will inevitably be full. Well, maybe not *actually* full, but with the only empty seats being directly next to someone else, so full for all practical purposes. Nobody sits directly next to someone at the gate – you need at least a one-seat buffer. Hell, a multiple-seat buffer is preferable, but that's usually wishful thinking unless you're at the gate five hours early. It's just a social norm thing; for whatever reason, we're uncomfortable sitting right next to strangers (even the people we might've accidentally swapped belts with back at security), so much that we'd rather stand or sit on the floor than rub elbows with some random. Next time you're at the airport, take a look; I guarantee there will be both open seats and people standing up.

After more waiting, we are finally ready to board the plane. A shrill woman with poor public speaking skills gets on the intercom and announces it's time for "pre-boarding," though I still haven't the faintest idea what this is. All I know is that I'm not allowed in it. One family and one old lady in a wheelchair get on the plane. Then she squawks out an invitation to board for first class travelers, as well as members of the delta premier, premier plus, and super duper premier-a-thon loyalty programs. These are the elites of air travel, and they get to board before us lowly peasants. Six or seven gentlemen with gel in their hair and cell phones on their cheeks wordlessly zip through the line. We continue to wait.

Soon we begin "general boarding," or boarding for the unprivileged in life. That's us. The intercom lady almost has a look of disgust as she says it – "GENERAL boarding," with an eye roll and small scoff. *What poor bastards* her eyes say as she announces the first few zones that are allowed to board. These first zones are not your zones. They are never your zones. You will continue to wait, and you will like it.

Finally the lowest of the low are allowed to get on the plane, and we walk in the jetway and encounter another line. We spend about 10 minutes looking at the floor in here, and eventually move to the actual plane, where we fight our way through legions of still-situating early-boarders and try desperately to cram our bag into what little space is left in the overhead compartment. It's a true struggle, but it always just fits. We find our seat between a moody child and a 300-pound man and try to get comfortable.

On the Plane

Finally, we are inside the vessel that will get us where we're going. Thus far, we've managed to avoid eye contact and conversations with the people near us, so despite the fact that this plane seems to have even less leg room than most, the trip is a net victory for the time being. We shove our second carry-on under the seat in front of us – hitting our head on the seatback in the process – and crack open a book, magazine, or cell phone game to kill time until takeoff.

Just when we're getting into the thick of our chosen medium, the flight attendants insist on doing their if-it-all-goes-to-hell demonstration. This is where they point out our seat cushions can be used for flotation devices, we should secure our own oxygen masks before assisting others, and even though oxygen is flowing, the bag might not inflate.

They force us to put down what we're doing and watch – kind of an ego trip, wouldn't you say? – but the demonstration is mostly irrelevant, because in the event the plane goes down, none of are going to remember one word of it. In the case of an air emergency, the cabin would not look

QUITTING COLD STONE (AND OTHER STRUGGLES)

like a uniform group of folks calmly implementing their safety training, but a hysterical mess of screaming and curse words. It's human nature to panic during an emergency, and while I've never been aboard a plane while it's going down, I have no doubt that's what would happen in this situation. Chaos would ensue, we'd discover the people seated in the exit row actually *aren't* qualified to carry out their exit row emergency duties, and some people might even help others with their oxygen masks before securing their own. In short, we'd all be screwed.

So honestly, I wish the flight attendants would be more practical about the whole thing. Something like this:

"The overwhelming odds are in favor of this plane reaching its destination without incident. If it *does* go down...well, that'll suck. But statistically, you're far more likely to be killed in an auto accident than a commercial aircraft, so we should be okay."

This would save a lot of time.

After the monologue, they also remind us that this is a non-smoking flight. Oh really? You don't say. Smoking has only been banned on every flight for the last 20 YEARS. Thanks for the heads up, and I'll put the Parliaments away.

Finally the airplane takes off, and the passengers rejoice* (*lay sideways in their seats and try to doze off). We of course aren't playing with our electronics at this point, because we were required to turn those off prior to takeoff. This is another airline farce; personal electronics pose no threat to airplane navigation equipment, which I am sure of because I always leave mine on. Whether it's because of forgetfulness (usually) or defiance (occasionally), I can't remember the last time I'm turned *all* of my electronics off on an airplane. Cell phone, sure – I don't really need that anyway, and it's quite possible that the satellite signal might actually do something negative. But mp3 players, iPads, laptops, and "anything else with an on/off switch," as the flight crew often jabs? I always leave at least one of them on, and I'm still here – never had an incident, never caused the plane to go down, never even had to use my seat cushion as a floatation device. I often travel with a coworker who deliberately waits until the flight attendants do their last pass, then fires up his iPad and watches a movie while the airplane ascends. His does this without fear of repercussions, because his wife – an air force pilot – once told him that the whole "all electronics must be off prior to takeoff" thing is complete horseshit. They only do it, she said, so you'll pay attention to their safety demonstration. I have no idea whether any of this is true, but so far the track record is perfect.

When the plane is in the air, I usually try to get a little nap in. Since there's nothing else going on, airplanes are a good place to catch up on sleep, even if it's just 20 minutes. So I lean my head back (or if the good Lord has seen fit to bless me with a window seat, against the window), and close my eyes as the plane continues its climb. Just as I'm about to doze, the captain's voice comes over the intercom. The fucking intercom.

Click [a bunch of loud unnecessary static nothingness before anyone says anything] [throat clear] Ahhhhhh...[another throat clear] Ladies and gentlemen, this is your captain speaking. We've...reached our cruising altitude of...[long pause while he remembers what the damn altitude is]...thirty thousand feet. We anticipate a smooth flight, and should have you safe and on time to your destination of...[another long pause while he figures out where the fuck he is flying the plane]...Dallas, Texas.

It's a casual, rambling, louder-than-necessary dialogue that gives you the feeling he had no idea what he was going to say before he turned the intercom on. He's just winging it, every flight of his life. His diatribe impeded my sleep the first time, but my eyes are still closed and I'm ready to doze again. I have a feeling he's not done, because the mic is still open, though he hasn't said anything in some 30 seconds. Perhaps it's over, and he just hasn't hung up the intercom yet. I begin to drift away. And then...

...Uhhhhh...I'm gonna go ahead and turn off the fasten seatbelt sign. Feel free to move around the cabin for the duration of the flight, but we like you to keep your seatbelt on when you are seated just for safety purposes. [15-second pause] We hope you enjoy the flight, and from me and the flight crew, I'd like to personally thank you for flying Air-Maxxx Airlines.

I'm wide awake. He ruined everything.

The duration of the flight is mostly peaceful, though every plane I've been on is in compliance with the federal aviation requirement that there must be at least one crying baby every three rows. We wordlessly put our headphones on and attempt to drown it out.

Finally the plane descends. And after the flight crew is completely satisfied that we can handle returning our seatbacks and tray tables to their full upright and locked position – and only after – the airplane can land. God forbid we touch down with someone's seat slightly reclined. Occasionally, once we've landed, someone onboard will applaud. I respond by throwing a bag of pretzels at their head, and everything's cool.

The second the wheels touch the ground, the passengers celebrate by immediately turning on their cell phones. It's a rolling thunder of startup noises and received texts. *Oh my god,* they must be thinking, *I've been off the grid for TWO HOURS. What have I missed? How have people coped with not being able to reach* me? *Should I just text everyone to let them know I'm okay? Probably. Group text...*

We've all become hopelessly phone-addicted, so once we get a few drought-breaking minutes with our digital best friends to calm the shakes, we resume waiting. And really, that's what air travel is all about: waiting. Waiting to check bags, waiting to get through security, waiting at the gate, waiting to board the plane, waiting for the plane to take off, waiting to land, waiting to exit the plane when it does land, waiting for our checked baggage (if we could stomach the $25), and waiting for our ride. We wait in one line for the privilege of waiting in another.

And at this point, we're in the "waiting to exit the plane" zone. As soon as the aircraft rolls to a stop at the gate, we hear a chorus of unbuckled seatbelts followed by everyone standing up. We're of course required to keep those seatbelts fastened until the plane has come to a complete stop, apparently to safeguard against injury if the plane hits something while taxiing at five miles per hour. Most travelers are remarkably compliant to this rule, and thus when we arrive at the gate the seatbelts all get taken off at once. The people cannot wait to get out of their seats and stand in place – awkwardly, while ducking the overhead bin – for 20 minutes. It's as if getting out of the seat will expedite the disembarking process.

Eventually the line begins to move and we *do* disembark – after, of course, we all take our sweet ass time getting our bags out of the overhead compartments. Then we can go.

Once we're off the plane, it's a mostly free-flowing 3-mile walk back through the airport. For the unlucky bastards that had to check a bag, there is still a 30-minute wait at the carousel and probably a lost piece of luggage in their future. The rest of us proceed to passenger pickup and get back on our cell phones to argue with our ride about the best meeting place. They've already been circling for an hour. We get in the vehicle and are forced to answer routine questions about how the flight was, and sometimes feign little details to paint some sort of unique picture, but in reality it's always the same. Once the ride is over, we'll be at our ultimate destination, and then – and only then – we can finally be alone.

QUITTING COLD STONE (AND OTHER STRUGGLES)

ABOUT THE AUTHOR

Sam Neumann is originally from Chisago City, Minnesota. He currently lives in Boulder, Colorado, where he is surrounded by mountains, organic food, and people with smartphones. This is his second book. You can find more about him and his current projects and rants at samneumann.com.